RUSSIAN JOKES, ANECDOTES AND FUNNY STORIES

Edward Dadiomov

To order additional copies of this book, contact:
Xlibris LLC
1-888-795-4274
www.Xlibris.com
Orders@Xlibris.com
64764

Contents

"It's a wonderful humor in this book but it's a pity that I speak neither English nor Russian".

—*Anonymous Writer*

"People will forget what you said.

They will probably forget what you did.

But they will never forget how you made them feel."

—*Unknown author*

Some say that beauty will save the world, others—that love will save the world, but it looks like humor will save the world.

Introduction

The book you are holding is my first one but I was trying to make it as funny, entertaining and amusing as possible for different groups of people speaking English. Between its covers you will find a lot of information that reflects Russian life in the form of humor.

In order to facilitate their finding, all jokes in the book are arranged in different chapters depending on their topics.

There are twenty five chapters in the book.

Chapters 'Advice', 'Famous People Speak', and 'Proverbs' do not completely match the subject of the book but most of the entries in these chapters contain a portion of humor, and hopefully they will also be interesting for readers.

Readers, if you find some of the jokes inappropriate or abusive, just ignore them.

It is well known that understanding foreign humor is often difficult for a number of reasons.

Moreover, it takes time to completely understand some jokes because of the nature of the humor.

Be patient please, and don't spend your valuable time trying to understand a joke if it is too hard.

LAUGHTER

And WHAT should be eaten in order to write such jokes?

Are you the last one to laugh? I'm behind you in line.

Laughter is not a sin at all if you laugh at something funny.

A smile is a curve to help set things straight.

Sleep and laughter is the best medicine, but not at the time when you have diarrhea.

—Is it true that one minute of laughter prolongs life up to five minutes?
—Well, it depends who you are laughing at . . . It can shorten your life as well . . .

Laughter is an instant vacation.

Laughter is one of the most infectious expressions of emotion.

Laughter is the soul's medicine!

Life is short!
Break the rules!
Forgive quickly!
Kiss slowly!
Love truly,
Laugh uncontrollably, and never regret anything that made you smile.

In every joke there is a bit of truth.

Solid humor is a massage for the heart.

Whether you know what Cain killed Abel for? No, not for what you've read in the Bible . . .
Because Abel, the Cain's brother, was telling old anecdotes. ☺

Humor is a very perishable product.

—The most sincere laughter is the gloating laughter!
—No, the most sincere laughter comes from being tickled!

If I understood all the jokes, I would have died of laughter.

The most sincere laughter is a malevolent laughter.

He who laughs last didn't get it at first.

Laughter is the shortest distance between two people.

—Victor Borge

What soap is to the body, laughter is to the soul.

—Yiddish Proverb

When people are laughing, they're generally not killing each other.

—Alan Alda

A man isn't poor if he can still laugh.

—Raymond Hitchcock

Man, when you lose your laugh you lose your footing.

—Ken Kese y

It was not a laugh but merely a loud smile.

—Author Unknown

Seven days without laughter makes one weak.

—Mort Walker

A laugh is a smile that bursts.

—Mary H. Waldrip

Laughter is the sun that drives winter from the human face.

—Victor Hugo

Laughter on one's lips is a sign that the person deep down has a pretty good grasp of life.

—Hugh Sidey

Laughter is the sensation of feeling good all over and showing it principally in one place.

—Josh Billings

Carry laughter with you wherever you go.

—Hugh Sidey

Laughter is a tranquilizer with no side effects.

—Arnold Glasow

Laughter is an orgasm triggered by the intercourse of sense and nonsense.

—Author Unknown

We do have a zeal for laughter in most situations, give or take a dentist.

—Joseph Heller

Perhaps I know best why it is man alone who laughs; he alone suffers so deeply that he had to invent laughter.

—Friedrich Nietzsche

Remember, men need laughter sometimes more than food.

—Anna Fellows Johnston

Advertisemets;
Announcements;
Inscrptions; Messages;
Slogans

ADVERTISEMETS

"**A**ntique tables! We make them daily!"

"**B**uy our wonderful beds!
Every tenth European is made on our bed!"

For Sale:
"Nerve system in excellent condition! It starts with a half-turn!"

"**F**rench cheese with mold! Cheese is from France and the mold is ours."

Travel Agency Ad:
"Unique trip across Europe on tank T-72. You pay for solar oil only!"

"**L**onely man will meet with a lonely woman to create a lonely child".

LOST DOG!
"Special features: boy of 7-8 years old is tied to the leash."

"We make a portrait of your enemy on toilet paper!"

For sale:
"German Shepherd from a good Jewish family".

Ad in kindergarten:
Dear parents! Please, do not believe all that your child tells you about kindergarten!
In return, we promise not to believe everything that your child tells us about you and your family!

Teeth? Our dentists will do everything to make you forget about them!

We make copies of all documents.
Originals are not required!

ANNOUNCEMENTS

"Those who have the swine flu are put on a strengthened ration with the increased contents of fodders".

"Young family (14 and 15 years old) searches for a family friend with a passport for buying alcohol and cigarettes".

Announcement in a Zoo:
"DO NOT FRIGHTEN the OSTRICHES! FLOOR is MADE of CONCRETE!"

A woman advertises in a newspaper:
"Please return the lost bag with my documents for decent or indecent compensation".

"Circus on Water' opened in Moscow!
Hurry up! Clowns are not able to float!"

"Experienced surgeon will help inexperienced men to dance well".

"There are no bad dancers in harem".

Federal program 'Accessible Residence':
"Make a few crimes and receive free residence for the term of 5 years!"

"Here is both some fragrant soap and a fluffy cord for you!"

"Crossbreed of a shark with a gold fish grants last three desires . . ."

"Dear buyers! Don't wash your hands in the aquarium, please!"

"Exchange displeasure of the day for pleasures of the night!"

"I'll pay $500 to those who can TEACH or DISACCUSTOM my neighbour to play piano!"

"In connection with work in your building the hot water supply will be stopped for a week.
For an additional expense we can stop the hot water supply in the neighbour building in order to not offend you . . ."

"Men! Do not be greedy! Give a starving child money for a pack of 'Camel' cigarettes!"

"We lay a mine in your car to prevent stealing! Phone us for a free estimate."

"New dental brush 'Oral-B' with cross-wise located bristles especially for your cross-wise located teeth!"

"Not very nice girl will get acquainted with . . . a set of cosmetics."

"Old and skilled kamikaze at your service!"

"The one who doubts our peacefulness will be washed with bloody tears!"

"Uneducated girl is searching for work on her speciality!"

"We are seeking a pleasant woman speaking FORTRAN, BASIC and C++ who will take care of an elderly programmer."

"I will buy the Faberge's eggs—both."
['eggs' also means 'testicles' in Russian slang]

"People! Protect nature otherwise it will become the environment."

Parachute for sale:
Used once, never opened, small stain".

"Lost a wallet with money. Return money at least!"

"Young man with an eyesight problem looks for a girl who is pleasant to the touch".

"I offer my hand and heart in exchange for the thighs and breast!"

"I want to quit smoking, so am looking for job in a warehouse of explosives".

"International dog show in North Korea.
With degustation".

Information board on the highway at the entrance to the city:
"Electric poles cause damage of your cars only in self-defense!"

Do you dream to dance on the stage of the 'Bolshoi'? I arrange a night 'show' for a small fee.
Security guard *Petrov.*

There are always fresh kidneys and livers in a canteen of a medical school.

"Meteorological center is seeking an individual with disease of the joints".

"Educated male, 34, very successful, smart, independent, self-made, looking for a girl whose father will hire me".

Male, 1932 model, high mileage, good condition, some hair.
Many new parts including hip, knee, cornea, valves. Isn't in running condition, but walks well.

INSCRPTIONS

If the inscription on your monitor's display is decreasing, they are carrying your computer off.

Inscription on a bottle of vodka: "Cool before abusing."

Inscription on a gravestone:
"You paid your taxes and now you can sleep easy!"

Inscription under a picture:
"Ass. Front View".

Inscription under a picture:
"Two species of fauna smoke a little of flora . . ."

Inscription on a tombstone:
"Here a known Odessa dentist *Katz Boris Raphailovich* is resting.
And his son *Monya* receives patients in his dental office on *Sovietskaya*, 21."

Inscription inside of a man's wedding ring:
"This rare woodpecker has been caught and rung in Moscow in 1995".

WRITTEN MESSAGES

"Mom! I'll be late and drunk tonight.
Your son".

On a restroom wall:

"Dear visitors! Do not throw cigarette butts in our urinals! We do not pee in your ashtrays!"

"This pathway isn't going to overgrow".

"The main thing is not to reach but to carry to".

"You're not going to leave anything good here".

Over the urinal in a restroom:

"Do not flatter yourself—come up to it closer!"

Over the toilet bowl:

"Gentlemen Pharaohs! Please flush your pyramids!"

Sign on a building wall:

"Family planning advice: Use rear entrance! Now that might work!"

On a tiger cage:

"Don't push your fingers through the cage! Penalty—one finger!"

Last will of a person suffering from claustrophobia:

"Bury me with a half-open coffin lid."

SLOGANS

"Greetings to participants of natural selection

Study, study, study once more, study once more, study once more, study once more . . . (computer virus: 'LENIN.exe')

[One of the most popular slogans of Vladimir Lenin: "Study, study, and study once more!"]

ADVICE

Take my advice. I don't use it anyway.

I never make the same mistake twice. I make it 5-6 times, just to be sure.

All is well if you do whatever you want within the Commandments and the Penal Code.

Are you ready to move mountains? So move your body from the couch!

Ask your doctor if Placebo is right for you.

Beer in the morning is not only harmful but also healthy.

Be not the one whose motive for action is hope for reward.

Be patient with everyone but above all with yourself.

Be ready to change your goals but never change your valuables.

Blow up your pair of lungs with illegal words . . .

Children are the flowers of life. Gift women the flowers.

Comrade, remember this! If you're wishing people health you want medical impoverishment!

Directions:
"When you reach the middle of the bridge make a right turn."

Dive into the Moscow-river, collect ten sticks of Koch and receive a mug of Esmarch as a gift.

Do more than hear, listen! Do more than listen, understand!

Don't argue with an idiot; people watching may not be able to tell the difference.

Don't marry a woman without whom you can live.
Marry the woman without whom you cannot live.

Don't save on a condom, or you'll lose on an abortion.

Don't show half-work to the fool.

Don't speak about yourself badly—people don't understand such jokes.

Don't ask me for advice! My sense of humor is stronger than my feeling of pity.

Don't cough and don't sneeze on another person's loaf.

Don't count the years—count memories!

Don't cut nails on your legs . . . they forecast an ice!

Don't dig a hole to another person—he/she will use it as an entrenchment.

Don't produce a strong sound wave. It can return in the form of a shock wave.

Don't eat! It can become a habit!

Don't go to a female monastery with a tired one . . .

Don't go searching for a mermaid if you don't know how to swim.

Don't hang on your moustache that which you hang on your ears.

Don't look at the traffic light while crossing a road—look at automobiles. Traffic lights have never forced down anybody.

Don't look in the holes of a free-of-charge cheese . . .

Don't put your payment in the business of others.

Don't tell me what I need to do and I won't tell you where you need to go.

Don't trust, be not afraid, don't ask. Come, take and carry away . . .

Don't try to live forever—it doesn't work.

Don't wait for opportunity to come; it's already here.

Don't wake me. I'm at work.

Don't wash your face anymore—it changes you.

Don't waste time on dirty tricks if you feel that you're capable of greater meanness.

Driver! Be careful at those places where children jump out!

Enjoy life now—it has an expiration date!

Even if you know that the mania of prosecution doesn't mean anything, somebody will pursue you.

First clean your soul and then—your teeth.

Forgive enemies, but in such a way that they cry!

From the rules of behavior in high society:
If someone called you "fool", do not be in a hurry to challenge them to a duel; maybe they just introduced themselves . . .

Good advice is no better than a poor one unless you follow it.

If you attach a bottle of vodka to the middle of a rope . . . pulling a rope will be much more exciting.

If your ideas seem ingenious to you, hide the bottle of vodka far away and go to bed.

If a person is deprived of a sense of humor, it means that he/she deserves it.

If a person shares apples it means that he has apples.
If a person shares ideas it means that he does not have apples.

If in the morning you do not desire to go to work, open 'Forbes' and find your surname there . . . Haven't found it? Then hurry to work!

If it didn't come out the first time, a parachuting sport isn't for you!

If it was possible for you to kick the person who's guilty in the majority of your troubles, you couldn't sit for a whole week as well.

If 'CAT' is written on a cage with a tiger, do not believe your eyes!

If someone does harm to you don't take it as an offence but give him candy; he harms you . . . and you give him candy . . . And so on until a diabetes forms in this creature.

If someone tells you that you are a many-sided person, don't be under delusion. He/she can mean that you are a reptile, a swine and a parasite at the same time.

If a child wasn't taught not to tell lies, he will grow as a politician.

If the third day of the week would not be desirable to work . . . so today is Wednesday.

If you are in the sea and feel that you begin to drown, urgently dial for help at: 847-537-1122 ext. 2357!

If you cannot change the circumstances, change your attitude towards them.

If you cannot overcome your weakness, convince everyone that it is your vital position.

If you can't afford a doctor, go to an airport—you'll get a free X-ray exam and a breast exam, and . . . if you mention Al Qaeda, you'll get a free colonoscopy.

If you have a problem, try to solve it. If you cannot solve it, then don't call it a problem.

If you missed your chance, never think that it is the last one; there will be more and more chances that you will miss.

If Mom thinks that you eat a lot and sleep a lot, it means that it is not your mother! It is her Mom!

If you woke up in the morning and there is a sensation that you have overslept for work, doze about an hour so this sensation grows in confidence.

If you open a '*matroshka*' (nested doll), seven or more corpses can be discovered.

If you pass by—pass by . . .

If you want your LAST word in a dispute, shoot yourself after you say it.

If you want the rainbow, you got to put up with the rain.

If you want your desires to come true instantly, carry a pistol with you.

If you want your dreams to come true, don't sleep.

If you want your husband to have a lot of money, do not take it away from him.

If you wish to win in a casino, buy a casino.

In order to cow eating less and give more milk, they should be less fed and more milk.

In order to find out what is going to be, you need to add up that what is now and that what has been . . .

It is almost impossible to cure sclerosis, but it is possible to forget about it.

It's about mind over matter: if you don't mind, it doesn't matter.

It's better to sit in a small, stuffy and dark beer house than to work at a big, light and spacious factory.

It's necessary to be able to use what you are given by God and to be pleased with what God did not give you.

It's not enough to know your own price; it's necessary to still be in demand.

It's not necessary to have friends; it's necessary to be friendly.

A joke repeated twice becomes more understandable.

Justice can easily be found in the dictionary . . . just look up the letter 'J' in the dictionary.

Learn the rules in order to break them correctly.

Let him who enjoys a good future waste none of his present.

It's better they laugh at you than cry!

Let's visit each other.
You visit me on a birthday, and I visit you on a funeral.

Look at everything as if you're seeing it for the first time.

Love all, trust few, do wrong to none.

Love books! They are not interrupted by advertisements!

Love cooking and prepare food with passion.

Love your enemies and they'll go crazy trying to understand what you're planning against them.

Never compromise a dream.

Never put off till tomorrow what you can do today.

Never refuse women—neither one, neither one!

Never tell your problems to anyone.
20% don't care and the other 80% are glad you have them.

Never trouble another for what you can do yourself.

No rules for success will work if you don't.

Nothing so warms your soul as a cold beer . . .

Personally, I invest in vodka! Where can you still receive 40%?

Plan ahead! It wasn't raining when Noah built the Ark!

Red wine is useful for your health. And health is necessary in order to drink vodka.

Remember! The Lord sees everything! Live so that it would be interesting for Him to watch!

Remember that the best relationships are those when your love for each other exceeds your need for each other.

Remember that silence sometimes is the best answer.

Secret of success in life depends on honesty and decency.
If you don't have these qualities, success is guaranteed!

Share your knowledge. It is a way to achieve immortality.

Speak! Speak! I always yawn when it is interesting to me.

Speak well of your enemies. After all, you made them.

Spend a part of every day alone.

The best contraceptive is still the word "No!"

Stop smoking, put on your skis and . . . instead of cancer there will be a hernia!

Strictly observing the rules of etiquette, you will leave malicious, sober and hungry.

Study, study, and study . . . because you are not going to find a job anyway.

Take care of a native land . . . have a rest overseas.

Take care of your character and your reputation will take care of itself.

The main thing in a drinking session—it shouldn't become bad earlier than good.

The more deeply you hide your head in sand, the more defenceless gets your ass.

The more you do that is not necessary, the more you receive that would not be desirable.

The secret of happiness? Grab a shovel.

The pen is mightier than the sword, unless you're up against a knight, then I suggest the sword.

—There is good medicine from love at first sight.
—What is it?
—Look the second time.

There is pleasure for the heart to play a dirty trick.

There is nothing more eternal than that which is wound by insulating tape.

To earn for a living it is necessary to work, but to grow rich it is necessary to think up something else.

To learn what will happen it's necessary to take into consideration what already is . . .

"Vodka in small portions is healthy in any quantity".

—M. Zhvanetsky

Want to know the truth? Read the multiplication table.

When someone tells you that nothing is impossible, ask him to dribble a ball.

When there's no choice, as a rule, the most correct decision is accepted.

When vodka comes to an end, the snacks become a simple meal.

When you lose something, please, don't lose your experience.

When your work speaks for itself, don't interrupt.

You'll manage to become a happy father if you'll be present not only at the birth of your child, but also at his/her conception!

You may know everything but not more.

Your character is what's left when you've lost everything you can lose.

You save a significant amount of money and time if it is a mutual love at first glance.

You should love your motherland so strongly that others would be afraid.

If you get lost in the Siberian forest, then scream as loud as possible. Thus, you save the *Ussuri* tiger that is listed in the Red Book.

If you are hit on the right cheek, then offer to hit the left one, and then hit the offender in the jaw.

Along with renaming militia to police, I propose to rename UAZ to JEEP, AvtoVAZ to Mercedes, and ruble to dollar.

If you are not glad with money, then it is not yours.

If you give your dinner to the enemy every day, he can become your friend.

In order for an answer to be positive, the question must be seducing!

Do not waste your time on petty tricks if you feel that you are capable of great meanness.

The best way to organize a panic: ask everyone to remain calm.

Always put off for tomorrow what you are never going to do.

Do not do anything on the first try, otherwise no one appreciates how difficult it was.

If you suddenly feel sad, think about an octopus. Its legs grow from its ears, its hands grow from its asshole, and its ass with the ears, and his head in its ass . . . and nothing is bad because it doesn't complain . . .

If you want to raise someone . . . buy a dog.

If someone rang the intercom and asked a stupid question, "Are you home?" don't be annoyed and just respond calmly, "Yes I am home, but where are you?"

Never say: "I made a mistake!" You should say: "I wonder why this is so interesting!?

If you want to make God laugh, tell him about your plans.

Love your wife! This is a reliable source of knowledge . . . of your weaknesses.

Do not steal! The government does not tolerate competition!

Counting money in someone else's pocket is ugly but interesting.

Beware of people who trust in God because they believe that God forgives them all.

Learn to appreciate those who cannot live without you, and do not chase those that are happy without you.

Eat your breakfast alone, share your lunch with your friend, and give your dinner to your enemy.
Eat your breakfast alone, share your lunch with your girlfriend . . . and you will forget about your dinner!

If a bank returns your check marked "Insufficient Funds," call them and ask whether they meant you or the bank.

Reading a newspaper while sitting on the toilet is reasonable because you're ready for any unexpected information.

Remember, when you communicate with people, they hear 80% of what you say, understand 60%, and memorize just 20%.

Be yourself! Just once a week!
And restore your reputation during the other six days!

If you think that the only food that makes you cry is an onion, then try to get hit on your forehead by a coconut.

Sometimes, someone calls and asks:
—Who's that?
I came up with an ingenious answer, which simply confuses the caller:
—Where?

The best way to end an argument with a woman is to play dead.

If a child begins to talk, it is too late to do an abortion . . .

A real Don Juan should wear less fashionable clothes to be able to dress as quickly as possible.

Eat breakfast yourself, share dinner with a friend, and give supper to your enemy doctor.

I think that you will not be wrong if you say nothing.

Remember, knowledge is not transmitted sexually.

Do you want to learn many new and interesting insights about yourself and your immediate family?
Drive your car in the far left lane at a speed not exceeding 30 km/h.

It is better to do something and regret than regret that you didn't do it.

If you have enough money, then you lack imagination.

If you have a beautiful wife, a good lover, cool car, no problems with the authorities and tax services, and when you go out on the street the sun always shines, and strangers smile—say NO to drugs!

If you think that nicotine does not affect a woman's voice, try to shake off the ashes on the carpet!

How to . . .
Patches of sunflower oil are easily derived by gasoline. Gasoline stains can be easily removed by an alkali. The spots of alkali disappear by applying vinegar. Traces of vinegar should rub by sunflower oil. Well, and you already know how to extract stains from sunflower oil.

If they lick your ass, do not relax! It is possible that this is just lubrication . . .

Don't make an elephant out of a fly!
You don't provide enough food for it!

To become a rich man you need three things: intelligence, talent, and lots of money.

Even if there are no chances, there is a chance that they will appear.

In order for cows to eat less and give more milk, they have to be less feed and more milk.

Do not take life too seriously—it is a temporary phenomenon . . .

Do not complain about life—it could not have been given to you at all.

Be a good parent! Remember, your kids will choose a retirement home for you.

If you get lost in the forest, then scream as loud as possible.
Thus, you do not give to die an Ussuri tiger listed in the Red Book.

Save time—fall in love at the first sight.

Do you want to enjoy the enigmatic smile of Mona Lisa, without visiting the Louvre?
Ask your wife how she spent your whole salary . . .

Don't boast that your wife is better than others—women might get offended, and men will want to make sure.

Boss And Secretary

A boss is interviewing a programmer, an engineer, and a secretary.

He asks what IQ they have.

The programmer:

—Well, somewhere near 140.

The engineer:

—About 120.

The secretary (proudly):

—90-60-90!

A boss says to a secretary:

"This letter is very important, therefore, place it near your nail polish so that we could find it at once when it is required".

A boss tempted a secretary for a while and at last she remained with him at the end of the work day. They were home late.

The boss was met by his wife with the question where he had been so late.

—Dear, I do not wish to lie to you, I tried to court our brand new secretary for a long time and today she finally allowed me to have sex with her. I was so tired that I fell asleep, therefore, I was late.

—Don't lie, villain! I see traces of grass on your shoes! You played golf after work again with your friends!

A boss is driving a car, and his secretary is sitting in the passenger seat. Suddenly the car breaks down. The boss thinks:

"As the boss, I should call road assistance, but as a man I should correct the breakage."

He gets out of the car and lays down under the machine. The secretary thinks:

"As a woman I should sit in the car but as a secretary I should be near my boss."

She gets out of the car and lays down under the machine. A policeman passes by:

"As a Frenchman I should go past but as a policeman I should warn them that their car has been stolen a long time ago."

—**A**nd where did your charming secretary disappear?

—I've dismissed her!

—Why? She is such a lovely girl!

—Yes, she is very lovely but she had an unpleasant laugh!

—It's strange because no employees noticed this.

—Well, nobody was present when I undressed . . .

A secretary is a girl who is paid for typing while she searches for a husband for herself.

A secretary should know and execute three commands very well: "Sit", "Lay", and "Fax".

A boss took his secretary on a business trip. He asks her in the evening:

—How are we going to sleep—like a husband with his wife or like lovers?

The secretary replies:

—Like a husband with his wife.

Then he turned to the wall and fell asleep.

A director steadfastly examines a new secretary.

"Four children", a personnel manager whispers in his ear.

"It cannot be. Such a young woman and she has four children already?"

"Not she, you."

Nothing spoils a family life like a personal secretary.

A sofa has been removed from the director's office . . .

The secretary, in amazement, asks her boss, "Should I consider myself dismissed?"

—**T**hrow away the cigarette!

—This is not a cigarette, boss, it's a pencil.

—Anyway, you cannot smoke in the workplace, even a pencil.

Two friends are talking by phone:

—I cannot meet with you ever, you're busy all the time.

—And did you try to arrange a meeting with my secretary?

—Yes, and we had a good time together, but, nevertheless, I wish to meet with you.

DIALOGS

Adam and Eve are walking in the Garden of Eden:
"Do you love me?" Eve asks him.
"Do I have a chance?" Adam says.

—Do you want it?
—Thanks.
—Thanks 'YES' or thanks 'NO'?

—Tell me, please, why the general on this monument in such a strange posture?
—Well, you know, an equestrian statue was conceived, but then they didn't have enough money for a horse.

—Why did your sister decide to become a dentist?
—Well, she likes when men look at her with an open mouth and wide eyes.

—Let's talk about beauty?
—Go ahead!
—Do you have hemorrhoids?
—No.
—So, this is fine!

—What time is it?

—I do not have a watch.

—And where am I?

—I also have no compass.

—David, what will happen if you break one of the Ten Commandments?

—Nine of them still remain.

—What is "good luck"?

—Well, this is when you walk down the street and a brick drops on your head.

—And if it falls next to me?

—Well, that is "bad luck".

—Do you like women?

—To be honest with you, I don't really understand them.

—Nobody understands them, neither Freud nor even themselves. It's like electricity. It is not necessary to understand it to have an electric shock.

—Dear TV program! Why do you constantly lie about the weather in our city?

—Why do you think the weather should be an exception?

—What are you doing at work?

—I want to go home!

—More than anything, I'm afraid of dentists and darkness.

—Why are you so afraid of darkness?

—Who knows how many dentists are in the dark!

—**H**ow is your son?

—Unfortunately, he doesn't know how to play cards.

—But this is a huge plus!

—It is rather a minus: he doesn't know how but still plays.

—**H**ello, is this the morgue?

—No, it is the bathhouse.

—I need the morgue!

—Wash yourself first . . .

—**T**his is from fatigue, this is from nervous breakdown and this is from depression.

—Thank you, doctor, thank you. And do you have anything but vodka?

—**D**on't you know what a stork does when it brings a baby?

—Oh, I know for sure, it turns to the wall and sleeps.

—**O**h, Mr. *Ivanov*, you've changed a lot! You used to be such a fat man and now you're so skinny!

—But I'm not Mr. *Ivanov*.

—Oh! You've also changed your name?

—**T**ell me, if I go to the right will there be a train station?

—It will be there even if you don't go there.

—**D**ear, did you hear that Peter's glands have been removed?

—Poor man, he wanted to have children so much!

—Your daughter is already married?

—Not yet.

—Why not?

—Oh, she is too smart to marry the idiot that will decide to marry her.

One Israeli general was asked: "Can you forgive a terrorist?"

He replied:

"God will forgive . . . Our task is to organize the meeting."

—Man! Buy a watch! Here is a replica of Swiss watch!

—I'll take it. Here is an exact replica of Russian money . . .

—What do you like best? Wine or women?

—It depends on the year it was 'manufactured'.

Lover resents:

—That's enough, I'm fed up! I'm tired of being second fiddle!

Mistress:

—Don't cry! Be thankful that you are in the orchestra!

Wife and husband:

She:

—I wish I could marry the devil.

He replies:

—Marriages between relatives are prohibited.

—You slept with him?

—Oh, come on! Just took a nap a couple of times . . .

You always kiss me on the cheek! You cannot find where else to kiss me?

—The child should be like his father!
—Fool! The child should be like a husband!

—I want a divorce.
—What are your reasons?
—There are many reasons. But most importantly, I'm married!

—The most important element in your diet for weight loss is a dream.
—How's that?
—Go to sleep on time, otherwise you overeat with pies!

Policeman stops a car:
—Your driver's license!
—Here you go . . .
—Did you know that you have a problem with the photograph on your driver's license?
—What is the problem? Here I am, third from the left?!

—The alarm was ringing?
—Yes.
—And what?
—It said that it will call back.

—You're so slim! Is this a new diet?
—Yes, carrots, beets and potatoes.
—Do you cook or fry them?
—I dig them!

—Do you drink?

—If this is a question—NO, if this is an offer—YES.

—Do you speak English?

—Only with the dictionary. I'm too shy with people.

—Does your wife cry during sex?

—No! She cries all the time but during sex she is very quiet.

"What coffin is the best?"

"It's hard to say", responses a seller. "The zinc coffin, of course, is more durable, but the wooden coffin is better for your health."

A phone call to the bank:

—Do you give credit to patients of the psycho-neurological clinic?

—Yes, but under a crazy percentage.

Waiter with a tray approaches a restaurant customer:

—Coffee or tea?

Client:

—Perhaps, coffee.

Waiter:

—That's a wrong guess—it is tea . . .

—Do you have a dream?

—Yes, I do!

—And what is it?

—I want to quit drinking.

—So, come on.

—And then how do I live without a dream?

—**I**'m taking your washing machine for repair.

—And what about me?

—You are beyond repair . . .

—**W**ho won World War II?

—You tell me who participated and I will guess . . .

—**B**urn the witch!

—But she is so beautiful . . .

—Well . . . then burn her thereafter!

—**L**isten, Holmes, why do all these Russians leave their country for London?

—Russians, my dear Watson, are very intelligent people. They do not live where they steal.

—**W**here are you going this summer?

—Well, probably to Siberia!

—Are you crazy?

—No, but the prosecutor insists!

—**H**ello! Hello! Help, I broke an arm.

—I'm a doctor, but a doctor of Law. You made a mistake, you need a medical doctor.

—I'm not mistaken. I broke someone else's arm.

—Mom, Mom, I want to go to the bathroom!

Mom (thoughtfully and dreamily):

—And I want to go to Paris . . .

A coach is consoling a losing boxer:

—You can scare your rival in the third round.

—How?

—He'll think he killed you.

—You know, the statistics say that every second a woman is unfaithful to her husband!

—Fuck your stats! I need the names, addresses, and phone numbers . . .

Little boy asks his father-meteorologist:

—Dad, are your predictions always correct?

—Always. Only the date doesn't always correspond.

—Excuse me, why do your famous burgers reek of vodka?

Waiter retreats a few steps and politely asks:

—And now?

What is the difference between true love and fake love?

Fake love:

—I like snowflakes on your hair!

True love:

—Fool, where is your cap?

A phone call at four o'clock in the morning:

—Hello! Is this Animal Cruelty Society?

Slow response of a sleepy man:

—Well, and who did you wrong, asshole?

—**A**re you dreaming of women?

—No, I'm not, because there is no time to sleep!

—**W**hy were you late for work?

—I left too late.

—And could you get out earlier?

—It was too late to leave earlier.

—**S**ir, you're a rascal! I challenge you to a duel! I give you the chance to choose a weapon: A sword or a gun?

—The sword!

—Excellent! Then I choose the gun!

Wedding:

—Will you marry this woman?

—No.

—And this one?

Two men meet each other:

—I'm getting married soon.

—And will you marry for love or for convenience?

—I do not know. My bride's father told me that I'll get married anyway.

—**I**s a biscuit healthier than a sausage?

—You know, now even smoking is healthier than the sausages.

Bob is out playing in the backyard, when his mother leans over from the window and yells:

"Bob, go home!"

The boy stops playing and asks—"Am I cold?"

The mother replies—"No, you are hungry."

—Waiter! May I have a cup of coffee?

—I am not a doctor! Ask your doctor if you can drink coffee.

At the market:

—Granny, what berry do you have?

—Black currant.

—And why are they red?

—Because they are green!

—When did you have sex last time?

—Last time did not happen yet!

—Will be there swine flu in Israel?

—Yes, but it will be strictly the kosher version!

—Hello, is this sex over the phone?

—Yes, and what do you want?

—What are you doing?

—Looking for my dog.

—Where did you leave it?

—In the *barking* lot.

—I saved your wife from being raped today.

—How?

—I persuaded her.

—I heard that you're going to marry?

—Yes, I am!

—And how do you like your future wife?

—Oh, so many men, so many opinions! Dad likes her, and I do not . . .

—Do the newspaper ads produce results?

—Of course! On Monday we placed the announcement that we're looking for a guard, and on Wednesday we were robbed.

One Caucasian centenarian was asked:

—What is the most unpleasant in longevity?

The highlander thought and replied:

—To watch how your grandchildren grow old.

—Mommy, can I go swimming in the sea?

—No way—see how the waves are!

—But Dad is swimming!

—He can, he is insured.

—My wife is happy in her marriage . . . And to discover the cause of this happiness, I hired two detectives.

—Why do I need a schedule of the trains, if they are always late?

—And how do you know that they are late, if there is no schedule?

—**W**hat do you call a woman who always knows where her husband is?

—A widow.

—**W**hat can you call your main achievement for having lived ninety-eight years?

—Perhaps, the fact that I have no enemies.

—That's great—not a single enemy!

—Yes, sir, I outlived all of them.

Waiter:

—Comrade, what will you order?

Client:

—I'd like a dish that eats the man sitting next to the window!

Waiter:

—Oh, it's absolutely impossible, he is almost done . . .

—**Y**our wife is noticeably thinner after her vacation. How has she achieved that?

—She is on the Chinese diet.

—Is it easy?

—She eats bouillon by wooden sticks for the whole month.

—**I**s there intelligent life in the universe?

—Yes, there is.

—And why haven't they contacted us?

—Because they are intelligent.

—**I**gor, I have a brilliant plan: Let's open a jewelry store together anywhere on Fifth Avenue.

—No, let's do it this way: you will open the store, and I'll stand down to ride . . .

—Lieutenant, you are a coward and a scoundrel! I challenge you to a duel!
—I'm not coming!
—Why not?
—Because I'm a coward and a scoundrel!

"Father Basil, why do so many people come to listen to preacher in church, there are a lot of youth, and they all look happy and smile?"
"So, that is the will of God", said Father Basil, stuffing hemp heavily into an incensory.

A foreign tourist asks a guide:
—What is the death rate in your country?
—The same as anywhere else. One death per person.

—Why did you marry your wife? She is not such a good-looking woman?
—She is very beautiful internally.
—So why don't you turn her inside out?

—Madam, it's a wonderful hat for you!
—It's too big in my opinion.
—Don't worry! There are two holes for your eyes in it!

Judge: Is there any reason you could not serve as a juror in this case?
Juror: I don't want to be away from my job that long.
Judge: Can't they do without you at work?
Juror: Yes, but I don't want them to know it.

—Sir, I don't think my present salary is commensurate with my performance!
—I know that, but I can't let you starve to death.

—Did you have any problems with your English in Canada, Ivan?
—No, I didn't have any; the Canadians did.

—Why do so many people believe in God?
—Because it is much easier to believe in the creation of the world described in the Bible, than understand the description of the same phenomenon by physicists.

—Does your husband still love you the same way?
—Oh, no. Luckily, he's learned something new.

—Hey, babe, what time is it?
—One hour—one hundred rubles!

—I've read so much about the harm that alcohol does to your body that, from now on, I've decided to quit.
—You've decided to quit drinking?
—No, reading!

—Let's meet tomorrow.
—OK.
—Where?
—Anywhere.
—When?
—Any time.
—Agreed. But please don't be late!

—Let me pound a nail into your head with this hammer, would you?

—No way! What if you were to miss the nail?

—Do you read newspapers?

—Yes, I do. Otherwise, how would I know that we live happy and prosperous lives?

—Excuse me, sir! Have you seen a policeman around?

—No, I haven't.

—Then give me your money!

—Such bluntness! I tell you in plain Russian that my wife is expecting a child and you're asking me who the father is?!

—I'm sorry. I just thought you might know.

—All men are womanizers.

—All of them?

—Oh, yes. You can't really call 'men' those who are not men.

—You're an idiot.

—I've never claimed to be otherwise.

A knock at the door at two o'clock in the morning:

—Open the door! We need to talk!

—How many of you are there?

—Just two of us!

—Then why don't you talk to each other!

A restaurant patron tells the waitress, "I'm so hungry, I could eat a dead rat!"
"Then you've come to the right place, sir."

—**W**aiter, there's a dead cockroach in my coffee!"
—So what do you want now, a funeral?"

"**C**an you make my horn sound louder?" a customer asks his mechanic.
"Why would you want to do that?"
"Well, I figured out that it'll be cheaper than fixing my brakes."

—**H**ello, is this an inquiry office?
—Wait, I'll find out . . .

—**I**'ve read so much about the harm that alcohol does to your body that, from now on, I've decided to quit.
—You've decided to quit drinking?
—No, reading!

—**L**et me pound a nail into your head with this hammer, would you?
—No way! What if you were to miss the nail?!

—**C**an you buy an honest person?
—No. But you can sell him.

—**S**omeone said that history repeats itself.
—Exactly! Once again, I have no money.

—**M**adam, can I invite you for a cup of coffee?
—You can, just do not smoke in bed!

A hotel's resident—an owner:

—Does your roof always leak?

The owner:

—No, sir. Only when it rains.

—What would you do if you get a million dollars?

—Return the debt.

—And the rest?

—The rest can wait.

—When I get married, many of my fans will be sad!

—Why many? You'll be married to just one of them.

During the celebration of the New Year, 2000 television reporters asked passers-by on the streets of London:

—What are your plans for this millennium?

Best answer:

—Pretty modest. Most of the millennium I will be dead.

—Hello! Is this a morgue?

—Yes, it is.

—If my mom calls tell her that I'm OK!

—Tell us, what forces you to drink vodka every day?

—Nothing. I'm a volunteer.

—What do you do if vodka interferes with your job?

—Quit the job.

FAMOUS PEOPLE SAY

There is no sincerer love than the love of food.

—B. Shaw

Humor is a rare condition of a talented person and a talented time when you are happy and smart at the same time.

—M. Zhvanetsky

Women are human beings who dress, chat and undress.

—Voltaire

It takes two people to marry: a lonely girl and a worried mother.

—Unknown Writer

Even the most beautiful legs end somewhere.

—Julian Tuwim

He loved her more than all the others but he needed others to make certain of this.

—Natalie Clifford Barney

Don't rush to your wife screaming "I know everything!" She then, God forbid, may ask you in what year was the battle of Trafalgar.

—"Pshekruy"

Do not follow after either a woman or a tram. More always come.

—Italian Saying

Men, who treat women with the highest reverence, rarely have their success.

—Joseph Addison

Of two evils choose the cuter.

—Carolyn Wells

Small world: in the end, we all meet up in bed.

—Brigitte Bardot

Always tell a woman that she is not like the others if you want to get from her the same thing as from the others.

—Wyndham Lewis

People have the right to engage in any sexual practice they like. However, they must avoid sex with goats.

—Elton John

Being a man is good because you do not need to kiss someone else's three-day stubble.

—Unknown Writer

The first kiss for a woman is the end of the beginning, and for a man—the beginning of the end.

—Helen Rowland

Sex is the most fun of all the things I could engage in without laughter.

—Woody Allen

I'm trembling for my country when I think that God is just.

—Unknown Writer

Health is when every day something aches elsewhere.

—*F. Ranevskaya*

German philosopher Immanuel Kant was asked:
"Which women tend to be more faithful, brunettes or blondes?"
Without thinking, Kant said:
"Gray-haired!"

My most brilliant achievement was my ability to be able to persuade my wife to marry me.

—Sir Winston Churchill

Socialism is a philosophy of failure, the creed of ignorance, and the gospel of envy, its inherent virtue is the equal sharing of misery.

—Sir Winston Churchill

A joke is a very serious thing.

—Sir Winston Churchill

Even if you are very talented and are making great efforts, some of the results just take time: you do not get a baby in a month, even if you make nine women pregnant . . .

—Warren Buffett

The one, who wants, does more than the one who can.

—Marie G.

The best way to help the poor is not to become one of them.

—Lat Hancock

Albert Einstein wrote to Charlie Chaplin:
Your films "The Modern Times" are a great success. Everyone in the world can understand them. You will certainly become a great man.
In the answer to Einstein's letter, Charlie Chaplin wrote:
I admire you even more. No one in the world can understand your "Theory of Relativity", but you have already become a great man.

Thomson (Lord Kelvin) was once forced to cancel his lecture and wrote on the blackboard: "Professor Thomson will not meet his classes today."
The students decided to make fun of the professor and erased the letter "c" in the word "classes".
The next day, checking the writing on the blackboard, Thomson kept his head, erased another letter in the same word and silently walked away.

"The hardest thing in the world to understand is income taxes."

—Albert Einstein

"Imagination is a quality given to man to compensate him for what he is not, and a sense of humor is a quality given to man console him for what he is."

—Oscar Wilde

"Be careful about reading health books. You may die of a misprint."

—Mark Twain

"Creativity knows how to hide your sources."

—Albert Einstein

"The reason I talk to myself is because I'm the only one whose answers I accept."

—George Carlin

"Reality continues to ruin my life."

—Bill Watterson

"I am free of all prejudice. I hate everyone equally."

—W.C. Fields

"The difference between genius and stupidity is: genius has its limits."

—Albert Einstein

"I'm not afraid of death; I just don't want to be there when it happens."

—Woody Allen

"Anyone who thinks sitting in church can make you a Christian must also think that sitting in a garage can make you a car."

—Garrison Keillor

"Never put off till tomorrow what may be done the day after tomorrow just as well".

—Mark Twain

"Two things are infinite: the universe and human stupidity; and I'm not sure about the universe."

—Albert Einstein

"You only live once, but if you do it right, once is enough."

—Mae West

"Everybody is a genius. But if you judge a fish by its ability to climb a tree, it will live its whole life believing that it is stupid."

—Albert Einstein

"When you are courting a nice girl an hour seems like a second. When you sit on a red-hot cinder a second seems like an hour. That's relativity."

—Albert Einstein

"I don't know the question, but sex is definitely the answer."

—Woody Allen

"I was gratified to be able to answer promptly, and I did. I said I didn't know."

—Mark Twain

"Fantasy is a necessary ingredient in living; it's a way of looking at life through the wrong end of a telescope."

—Dr. Seuss

"My tastes are simple: I am easily satisfied with the best."

—Winston Churchill

"I always arrive late at the office, but I make up for it by leaving early."

—Charles Lamb

"What would men be without women? Scarce, sir . . . mighty scarce."

—Mark Twain

"Have you ever noticed that anybody driving slower than you is an idiot, and anyone going faster than you is a maniac?"

—George Carlin

"Black holes are where God divided by zero."

—Albert Einstein

"I have nothing to declare except my genius."

—Oscar Wilde

"I never forget a face, but in your case I'll be glad to make an exception."

—Groucho Marx

"The secret of life is honesty and fair dealing. If you can fake that, you've got it made."

—Groucho Marx

"Learn from the mistakes of others. You can never live long enough to make them all yourself."

—Groucho Marx

"In the beginning there was nothing, which exploded."

—Terry Pratchett

"The covers of this book are too far apart."

—Ambrose Bierce

"Those are my principles, and if you don't like them . . . well I have others."

—Groucho Marx

Aphorisms by Kozma Prutkov:

"Throwing pebbles into the water, look at the ripples they form on the surface. Otherwise this activity will be an empty amusement."

"Where is the beginning of the end that comes at the end of the beginning?"

"If you have a fountain, shut it down. Let even a fountain have a rest."

"If you see a "buffalo" sign on an elephant's cage, do not trust your eyes."

"If ever asked: What's more useful, the sun or the moon, respond: The moon. For the sun only shines during daytime, when it's light anyway, whereas the moon shines at night."

"Nobody can take hold of limitless."

"When it concerns art, every tailor has views of his own."

"Every expert is like a gumboil: his fullness is one-sided."

"Not every general is stout by nature."

"God placed death at the end of life to give us time to prepare for it."

"If you want to be happy, be so."

"If you want to be handsome, enroll in the Hussars."

"Diligence overcomes everything!"

"Sometimes, diligence can overcome even reason."

"Don't tell jokes to ladies, for these jokes are stupid and obscene!"

"Even an oyster has enemies."

Woman inspires us to great things . . . and prevents us from achieving them.

—Dumas

I've been married to a communist and a fascist, and neither would take out the garbage.

—Zsa Gabor

After the game, the King and the Pawn go into the same box.

—Italian proverb

When a man opens a car door for his wife, it's either a new car or a new wife.

—Prince Philip

Lawyers believe a man is innocent until proven broke.

—Robin Hal

Kill one man and you're a murderer, kill a million and you're a conqueror.

—Jean Rostand

We are here on earth to do good unto others. What the others are here for, I have no idea.

—W.H. Auden

FOR BOYS ONLY

A boy was trying to explain by gestures that his name is Dick.

A boy pesters a girl:
—Girl, may I teach you the art of love . . .
—And how much are you going to spend on my education?

All people are as people. And I—I'm as beautiful as God!

—Are you smoking? What class?
—Bourgeoisie.
['class' means both 'grade' and a 'social group' in Russian]

Beautiful girls are hit on the head with a portfolio by boys in the elementary grades, and then people are surprised why almost all of them become silly women.

Come on in! Lie down! Hello!

Confess, what girls do you like more—clever or beautiful?
Neither! I need YOU only!

Conversation over the phone:

—Hello! Good evening, *Irina Nikolaevna*.

—Hi, *Egor*, are you looking for *Sveta*? She cannot talk right now because she is taking a shower.

—Yes, yes . . . I know. Could you, please, bring two towels for us here?

—Daddy, I have a problem with our new teacher.

—Well, *Vovochka*, problems can be solved. Be engaged, be attentive at lessons, do your homework on time . . .

—I don't think that it's going to help. She told me that she has a critical day delay for four weeks already.

—Do you love me?

—Yes, certainly! And you?

—Oh, I love myself too!

Do you want me to explain this with fingers? Are you seeing the middle one?

Eventually I understood: nobody can find anything better than a wife.

So, there remained only to find a wife.

Excuse me, but I imagined you completely different when I saw you on the dating site.

I met a wonderful girl but her parents are against our happiness. They want me to marry her . . .

It is impossible to take my eyes off her when I'm ten steps away.

In two steps away . . . it is already possible!

It is too bad without girls but it is still good . . . If it is good without girls, it is really bad.

—Girl! And what will be if I kiss you?

—Have you studied anatomy? Nothing will be! Nothing!

—Girl! Are you still studying or do already know how?

—Girl! Do you dance?

—No.

—Then, let's not waste our valuable time!

—Girl! Do you wish to begin romantic relationships with somebody?

—Yes, I do!

—OK! I'm Roma!

Girl!

If I were a poet, I would devote poetry to you!

If I were an artist, I would have drawn your portrait.

But I'm only a security guard at a furniture factory, so I can offer you a bed.

I have fatally wanted to sleep but there was nobody to sleep with . . .

—Ivan! Would you buy me these flowers!

—Why? You're still alive!

Maybe you need a key from an apartment where girls squeal?

My girl is not any worse than others. So why do I like others much more?

One head is good . . . but the whole body is better.

One word at the wedding—and you're married. One word in the dream—and you're divorced.

Puzzle:
Katya has two apples, and Lena—two melons. Which girl is more attractive?

She was so beautiful that she could be neither smart nor kind.

—Stop thinking about it, honey. I'm not going to let you do it before the wedding.
—In that case, give me a call after the wedding!

Telephone is ringing. *Ivan* picks up a phone and listens to the woman's voice on the other end of the phone line:
"Dear, I'm going to tell you very good news—I'm pregnant!"
There's a deep silence for about fifteen seconds and then:
"Wrong number, wrong number . . ."

—Tell me, Alexander, and did you have sex before you met me?
—No.
—And you won't now as well!

The best four-legged friend is a bed!

Transitional age is the age when you understand what you do want: an ice cream or a beer during hot weather.

Two friends meet each other:

—Listen, do you love group sex?

—Yes, I do.

—So, go home. They need more people.

—What are you going to drink: champagne, beer, wine, vodka?

—Yes, perhaps, I will drink in such an order.

—Who are you?

—I'm Sleeping Beauty.

—And why are you so terrible?

—Just woke up but haven't used my cosmetics.

Yesterday I got acquainted with a beautiful girl in a nightclub!

She told me: "Let's have a baby!"

And I told her: "Well let's. Why should a child be frozen in the street?"

FOR GIRLS ONLY

The difference between a decent girl and an indecent girl: you never know how much it will cost you.

A girl's prayer before a dream: "My God, save and protect me . . . against pregnancy!"

A guy phoned his girlfriend:
—Why didn't you pick up the phone so long?
—I was dancing to the music of the telephone ring . . .

A man never feels as weak as at the moment when a pretty girl starts to say that he is strong.

Advice for girls:
Black shoes on a flat sole match a bald and low man.

—And does your groom know how old you are?
—Yes, partially . . .

—And what are you doing this evening?

—Nothing.

—Search for a job! She does nothing!? Go! Your work is necessary for the country!

Are you the daddy of my child too?

Blondes carry sun glasses on their hair because if they put them on their nose it becomes dark and terrible.

Both Mother and the Ministry of Health warned . . .

Dad, I'm pregnant . . . Here's a list of suspects.

—Daughter, people say that you slept with your groom already.

—People will tell you, listen to them more! If I slept with somebody, do they consider him a groom?

Don't cry, my darling, don't cry! We'll find a man for you.

The duration of marriage is inversely proportional to the expenses for the wedding.

Formerly girls reddened when they were ashamed, and now they're ashamed before they redden . . .

Gee! Don't cry so . . . You're the most favorite and the most unique from all of them . . .

—**G**irl, and does your Mom need a son-in-law?

—No.

—And a drinking companion for your daddy?

—**G**irl, are you resting alone or with your girlfriend here?

—With the boyfriend of my girlfriend.

—**G**irl! Do you like to dive?

—Yes, I do.

—Then let us dive under a blanket.

Girls are divided in two categories: those that love the men capable to drag a refrigerator to the fifth floor without an elevator, and those that love the men capable of paying for work of the men from the first category.

Girls! Curved legs do not spoil a figure . . . if you're bald, thick, malicious, and a silly woman.

Girls do not have enough femininity, and women—virginity.

Girl enters a sex shop.

—Please give me that black, that green and that red.

—Well, I'll give you the black and the green. But about the fire extinguisher you should talk to the manager!

Girl, what beautiful hair you have! I would even say—rare! Very rare/sparse hair . . .

—Girl, what phone do you have?

—Motorola.

—No, I mean the number?

—Federal.

—No, what are the figures?

—Arabic.

Girl, you smell so good . . . What did you drink today?

—Greetings! What a pretty blouse!

—Imagine, there is nothing under it!

—Don't worry, they will grow!

Having seen her I stood up but partly . . .

How many good girls dream about bad, secretly?

—I apply for your heart . . .

—It's a pity but I've already undressed . . .

I don't know what an interview is but I'll take another wash for any case.

If a girl has tits, has time and has milk so why not feed a child.

If you have again gained five kilograms during a week it means that this diet has been advised to you by your best girlfriend.

—May I call you Boeing?

—Why?

—Because you're my 747th.

I looked out of the window in the morning and there was a message written in large letters on asphalt: "I love you, *Rita*!",—on the very place where my car is usually parked.

I don't look bad . . . but not very often.

I'm like the Universe. I'm awfully lonely . . .

I'm not an honors pupil. I'm satisfactory!

I'm not a street girl! Let's go to an entrance . . .

It's easy to be beautiful but it's difficult to inspire it in others.

—Kiss me in a token of an armistice.
—And where is it?

Law of nature:
If a girl lost consciousness there will be always a man who loses conscience.

—Listen, you're very short-sighted, why do you always take off your glasses when your fiancé shows up?
—Well, first, I'm much prettier without glasses, and secondly, my fiancé is much more handsome when I'm without my glasses.

Long legs are not a luxury but the means of moving.

—Man, are you bored?
—Not very . . .

Men come and go, and the earrings remain.

Morning. A girl enters a drugstore. She is very tired and asks a salesman: "Give me something from spermatozoa, please . . ."

No, I cannot lie in this pose before the wedding.

One million scarlet roses were presented to a girl . . .
And she said that if an even number of flowers was given, it means that you wish her death. She turned around and left.

Our motto is invincible—we excite and do not give!
[to 'give' means a female permission to have sex with her (Russian slang)]

Strict daddy—to his daughter:
—*Masha*, I saw how you made love with a young man in his car yesterday. Who was he?
—What color was the car?

The best girls' decoration is modesty and a transparent dress.

The shorter a skirt—the more flaws it hides.

The word "NO" is still the best contraceptive.

The most attractive girls are there where men drink a lot.

Two girls communicate:

—I have a delay for four months.

—Are you pregnant?

—No, I'm waiting for the pay check!

Two guys look at a girl.

—The girl's legs are like gazelle legs.

—What, slender?

—No, hairy.

Two young women are talking:

—I'm going to marry the man I fall in love with.

—I will too, if I don't find anybody better.

What a beautiful leg you have . . . And where's the second one?

—What is in common in a mini skirt and a yashmak?

—Both help ugly girls to hide their faces.

—Why do girls always look down when guys tell them about their love?

—Just to see it's true . . .

—Will you come to my wedding?

—When?

—On Friday.

—And who will you marry?

—You.

—Then I shall come.

Young man, take your hand off my knee right now! I will begin to count up to five . . . thousand!

A girl with deep cleavage came to confess to a priest. The priest looks at her neckline and says,
"Oh, my God!"
Voice from heaven: "Well, you finally called me to take a look at what is worthwhile!"

Women can do everything, but some are shy.

If there is a sex-bomb—there should be a sex-bomb shelter.

Mother's parting words before the wedding:
—Daughter, never argue with your husband! Immediately cry!

—How do bring your girl to a madness?
—Give her a lot of money and close all the stores!

Girls with small breasts, do not worry! Now you know for sure that your guy likes you for your eyes.

—Do you believe in love at first sight?
—No.
—Then look at me again.

"Who are these men?" a young fellow asks his girlfriend when he sees an entire wall pasted with pictures of men. "Your ancestors?"
"No," she replies, your predecessors."

FOR MEN ONLY

—Who is more satisfied: a man who has six children, or one who has six million dollars?

—Man who has six children!

—Why?

—Man with six million wants more!

—Man, will you accompany me home?

—I'm going to just follow you with my eyes, madam.

You will be ashamed of me but not bored . . .

A smart man always knows what he wants but a wise man also knows why he wants it.

Man's logic forces me to rely on women's intuition.

What is "success"?

At 4 years, if you do not pee in your pants

At 12 years, if you have friends

At 20 years, if you have sex

At 35 years, if you earn a lot of money
At 60 years, if you have sex
At 70 years, if you have friends
At 80 years, if you do not pee in your pants

It is easy to take away another man's wife but it is difficult to get her back.

It's easy to make women happy . . . but expensive.

A man chases a woman until she catches him.

There're no ugly women—there're men who are cowards.

She followed him to Siberia and spoiled all his hard labor.

Woman usually doesn't pay much attention to a handsome man but to the man with a beautiful woman.

If in the arms of your wife you dream about someone else's wife then you're male and lecher.
And if in the arms of another's wife you dream about your own wife you're a great family man.

Married men live painfully longer . . .
Women are the same as we are . . . only more pleasant to touch.

A striking resemblance of women and men should not mislead you.

It's always difficult with a beautiful woman—you either see her in your dreams or you just do not sleep . . .

In some males the major hemisphere is protected by the skull, in others—by the pants.

Bachelors do not realize how happy it is to be married. Married men do not understand it as well . . .

If you met the woman of your dreams, you can say goodbye to the rest of your dreams.

Some women are so shy that they are embarrassed to reject men.

The main reason for heart attacks in men over 60 are women under 30.

Man's logic:
Are you cold? Hold me tight.
Are you hot? Undress . . .

In his 20 years, he knew six operating systems and no women.

If a woman turns on her left turn signal, it does not mean that she is going to make a right turn. She can go straight.

All males are divided into those who see a woman as a person, those who do not see a woman as a person, and those who see a woman in every person.

She used to be the woman of my dreams until I learned the dreams of my woman.

When a man feels bad, he is looking for a woman.
When a man feels good, he is looking for one more.

If a man is willing to do anything for a woman, that means he loves her.
If a woman is ready to do anything for a man, that means she gave him a birth.

—Now, like a real man, you just have to marry me!
—Madame, like a real man, I'm already married!

You should never trust a woman who doesn't conceal her age. The woman who can do this is capable of anything!

A picture after sex looks like the one after a battle: a woman moans like she's wounded, and a man falls asleep like a dead person.

The only real drawback of group sex is that you can disappoint two women instead of one.

Do not look for a woman's soul. Be satisfied by her body.

—Why will a real man never marry a real woman?
—Because the real woman will never accept the man's offer the first time!
And the real man will never offer twice . . .

Every woman is a mystery. You never know how much she will cost . . .

When a man is bad, he is looking for a woman. When a man is good, his wife is looking for him.

The fact that men lie, should be addressed to women, because they ask too many questions.

He was ready to give up his life for love, but she took only cash.

—Tell me, colonel, what hobbies did you have in your youth?
—Women and hunting!
—And what did you hunt for?
—Women.

Have you ever wondered why it takes MILLIONS of sperm and only one egg to make a baby? It's because not one of those little surfers will stop and ask for directions!

Men always want to be a woman's first love, women like to be a man's last romance. (Oscar Wilde)

Psychoanalysis is a lot quicker for men than for women because when it's time for a man to go back to his childhood, he's already there.

Women take clothing much more seriously than men. I've never seen a man walk into a party and say, "Oh no, I've got to get out of here. There's another man wearing a black tuxedo."

An English professor wrote the words, "Woman without her man is nothing" on the blackboard and directed the students to punctuate it correctly.

The men wrote: "Woman, without her man, is nothing."

The women wrote: "Woman! Without her, man is nothing."

Don't marry for money; it's cheaper to borrow it.

I love you more today than yesterday—yesterday you really got on my nerves.

I'd like to live life in the fast lane but I'm married to a speed bump.

If you made a list of the reasons why any couple got married and another list of the reasons for their divorce, you'd have a lot of overlapping!

Love is a gross exaggeration of the difference between one person and everybody else.

—George Bernard Shaw

Love is the quest, marriage is the conquest, and divorce is the inquest.

The thing that takes up the least amount of time and causes the most amount of trouble is sex.

Where there is marriage without love, there will be love without marriage.

—Ben Franklin

Whenever I date a guy, I think, is this the man I want my children to spend their weekends with?

—Rita Rudner

Women don't make fools of men—most of them are the do-it-yourself types.

You have two choices in life: You can stay single and be miserable, or get married and wish you were dead.

He loved her more than all the others, but he needed others to verify this.

Q: Why are women worse than the mafia?
A: The mafia demands money or your life; women want both.

All should be perfect in woman: the soul, the mind, and everything you're currently thinking about.

FOR STUDENTS ONLY

19-th century. St. Petersburg University.

Professor asks the late student:

—*Raskolnikov*, why are you so late?

—Yes., here, the old woman . . .

—Did you help her to cross the street?

—No, I took her farther!

A polar bear is a rectangular bear after the transformation of coordinates.

A silly university entrant pays a tutor, and a clever one—an examiner.

A student asks the librarian:

—Excuse me but I asked you about the newest anatomy textbook and not about this twenty year old book. Do you really have nothing newer?

—Do you really think, young man, that in the last years the design of the human skeleton has been changed?

Exam on language.

—Take a ticket, please. What is your ticket's code?

—Code . . . It . . . "C" would be fine . . .

The exam is passed brilliantly. Professors are delighted. They ask the student to repeat it in the autumn.

Fermat's last theorem would proven a long time ago if it was included in the examination ticket.

Give a student a point of support and he will fall asleep . . .

During student times we lived in a dormitory and there was a piece of paper fastened to the door of our room with the warning: "Dear Moms and Dads! Remember that an unexpected knock on the door can make you grandmothers and grandfathers".

Medical college, a gynacology faculty. Professor addresses the sophomores: "Every student should have a girlfriend. You cannot do your homework without her".

Professor asks a student:
—What is necessary to change to make Russian cars meet the demands of world standards?
Student's answer:
—World standards.

Student badly answers questions at an examination. Professor asks him:
What is an examination in your opinion?
It is a conversation between two clever people.
And if one of them is an idiot?
Then the second one will not receive the scholarship.

Student is not ready for exam in two cases:
1. If he has not taken an exam yet.
2. If he has already taken an exam.

Student:

—I don't think I'll pass this exam . . .

Professor:

—I bet you $100 that you will!

There was a competition among students of one college for the best short story. There could be any topic with four necessary conditions:
1) There must be a queen in the story
2) God must be mentioned
3) A little sex
4) A mystery should be present

The first prize was awarded to a student who could fit the story in one sentence:

"Oh, my God!"—exclaimed the queen. "I'm pregnant and do not know by whom!"

"Why do you worry so much?" the professor asks his student before the exam. "Are you afraid of my questions?"

"No, professor," the student explains, "I'm afraid of my answers."

Yesterday a drunken professor was demonstrating electromagnetic waves during his lecture.

Graduate *Sidorov* at the exam in literature significantly enriched the meaning of the famous sayings of Socrates: "I know that I know nothing",— by adding: "And I do not want to know!"

The computer says I need to upgrade my brain to be compatible with its new software.

List of answers from test papers submitted to science teachers by elementary, junior high, high school, and college students: It is truly astonishing what weird science our young scholars can create under the pressures of time and grades. The spellings are the original ones.

1. H_2O is hot water, and CO_2 is cold water.
2. To collect fumes of sulphur, hold a deacon over a flame in a test tube.
3. When you smell an odorless gas, it is probably carbon monoxide.
4. Water is composed of two gins, Oxygin and Hydrogin. Oxygin is pure gin. Hydrogin is water and gin.
5. A super saturated solution is one that holds more than it can hold.
6. Liter: A nest of young puppies.
7. Magnet: Something you find crawling all over a dead cat.
8. Momentum: What you give a person when they are going away.
9. Vacuum: A large, empty space where the pope lives.
10. Artificial insemination is when the farmer does it to the cow instead of the bull.
11. The pistol of the flower is its only protection against insects.
12. A fossil is an extinct animal. The older it is, the more extinct it is.
13. To remove dust from the eye, pull the eye down over the nose.
14. For a nosebleed: Put the nose much lower that the heart until the heart stops.
15. For head colds: use an agonizer to spray the nose until it drops in your throat.
16. Germinate: To become a naturalized German.
17. The tides are a fight between the Earth and moon. All water tends towards the moon, because there is no water on the moon, and nature abhors a vacuum. I forget where the sun joins in this fight.
18. Blood flows down one leg and up the other.

—

A student is floundering during an exam. "Your mind is like a desert, sir," the professor tells him in frustration.

"Every desert has an oasis, professor," the student replies. "But not every camel is able to find it."

For Women Only

Every woman wants a new dress, but more than that she is wants to fit into the old one.

Women begin with resistance to an offensive from men, and end up by standing in the way of retreat.

When a woman has nothing to say, it does not mean that she will be silent.

Even if at some point a woman is satisfied then quickly comes a moment when she begins to be dissatisfied with the fact that she was satisfied with everything.

Beauty is a terrible force!
Beauty requires sacrifice!
Beauty will save the world!
How can a terrible force that requires sacrifice save the world?

Only a random number generator can argue with female logic.

If you seduced a man then, as an honest woman, you have to marry him! And there is no reason to feel sorry for him!

Female intuition is a good thing . . . until female logic comes . . .

If a woman suddenly stopped talking then she has something to say.

Why does everyone say that women love money? We don't like it! Look at the speed with which we get rid of it!

I look at myself in the mirror and see a beautiful woman! Look more closely . . . Damn . . . GODDESS!

Kids want to look older. Men want to look smarter. And women—younger and more foolish.

How should I live?! Nobody wants me except my husband.

Eternal feminine problem:
How to distinguish a good man and a bad man if both want the same from you!?

—Madam, what do I have to give you to get your love?
—Anesthesia.

Woman wants everything from one man. Man wants one thing from every woman.

For a woman, old age comes when the TV becomes more interesting than the mirror . . .

There is a man—there are a lot of problems. There is no man—there is one problem: NO MAN!

An experienced woman is a woman who knows how to pretend to be inexperienced.

—Is it possible for a Russian woman to live on her own salary?
—It is, providing she dresses herself on credit and undresses for cash.

The great question that has never been answered, and which I have not yet been able to answer despite my thirty years of research into the feminine soul, is: "What does a woman want?"
—Freud

Intuition: that strange instinct that tells a woman she is right, whether she is or not.

Not all men are annoying. Some are dead.

What's the fastest way to a man's heart?
Through his chest with a sharp knife.

Why did God put men on earth?
Because a vibrator can't mow the lawn.

—Why did God make man before woman?
—You need a rough draft before you make a final copy.

You have the right to remain silent, so please SHUT UP.

She was so beautiful that she could be neither wise nor kind.

A woman is explaining what kind of man she wants to meet at a dating service:
"He has to be polite, he has to have various interests, he has to know how to have a good conversation, he has to know what's going on around the world, and he has to never interrupt me."
"You don't need a man, madam, you need a TV!"

HISTORICAL JOKES

A famous physiologist *Ivan Pavlov* was bitten by a dog in his childhood . . . The dog grew up and forgot that. But *Pavlov* has grown up and has not forgotten.

Alexander Makedonsky, on the beach of the Mediterranean Sea, noticed Diogenes lying on the sand and tanning under the sun. He approached him and asked:
"I didn't expect to meet a famous Greek philosopher here. Let me fulfil any of your wishes."
Diogenes turned to him and replied:
"You know, don't obstruct the sun, please, I'm taking a sun bath".

Ancient Kirghizs did not know about Jews, therefore all natural disasters were attributed to the dark forces of nature.

A well-known Russian writer *Leo Tolstoy* could do almost everything he wanted with *Natasha Rostova*.

Historians confirm that inquisitors burned the witches not because they hated them but because they were lacking a woman's warmth.

In the USSR all has been done through the ass except for an enema.

L.I. Brezhnev was appropriated the next military rank of the Marshal of the Soviet Union. Before his death his inferiors were going to appropriate him the rank of the Generalissimo but then they changed their mind as he wasn't able to pronounce that word.

L.I. Brezhnev was asked a question:
"Will there be money in the time of communism?"
L.I. Brezhnev answered:
"There will be money in the time of communism but not everyone will have it."

Nikita Khrushchev, after visiting the United States, decided to change the layout of apartments for the families of the Soviet Union. He proposed to combine a bath with a toilet in one space. The Russians made a joke that pertains to this situation: "Nikita managed to combine a bath with a toilet, but he did not have time to join a ceiling with a floor.

Remember what Archimedes said in his Doric speech of Syracuse:
"Give me a place to stand and with a lever, and I will move the whole world."
There was a resolution of the ancient Greek official: "Reject Archimedes in his request for granting a point of support because he will overturn something else."

Small Nostradamus asks his mother:
—Mom, what do we have for dinner today?
—I'm sure you know, a little shit.

Josef Stalin and Marshal *Zhukov* discuss a plan for a strategic operation:
Stalin: "Well, and what will comrade *Zhukov* say?"
Zhukov: "And what will comrade Stalin say?"
And on and on until the morning . . .

The citation from the latest Ukrainian history textbook:
"The Russian barbarians rushed into Ukrainian cities and villages leaving behind the built libraries, universities and theatres."

Vladimir Lenin loved kids very much but his first arrest was for political activity.

—When did the Great Britain judges start to wear black clothes?
—They began to put them on for the mourning of Queen Victoria.
—But why do they wear them now?
—Because, in fact, she is still dead!

—Did you know that Robin Hood took money away from the rich and gave it to the poor?
—And how did he live?
—He lived off of the interest!

Yalta Conference, 1945.
Churchill was sent a written message. He read it, burned it by his cigar and sent his reply back.
The sender read it, then tore it up to pieces and threw it in the waste-paper basket.
But *KGB* agents picked it up from the basket and restored the original text:
"The old hawk isn't going to fall out of the nest".

The KGB could not understand the text then . . .

Later when *Nikita Khrushchev* was in Great Britain, he met with an elderly Churchill and asked him (because many years already passed) what was the meaning of the note.

Churchill answered that the sender let him know that he had an unzipped pants zipper.

Husband And Wife

A bachelor does all the work on the house by himself. And a married man is forced to by his wife.

After twenty four years spent with my wife I understood that she became my close relative . . .
And now any opportunity for sex with her I consider as incest.

A husband and a wife are equal in rights in the family—especially the wife.

A husband and his wife are sitting quietly in bed reading when the wife looks over at him and asks the question . . .
W: "What would you do if I died? Would you get married again?"
H: "Definitely not!"
W: "Why not? Don't you like being married?"
H: "Of course I do."
W: "Then why wouldn't you remarry?"
H: "Okay, okay, I'd get married again."
W: "You would?" (with a hurt look)
H: (makes audible groan)
W: "Would you live in our house?"

H: "Sure, it's a great house."

W: "Would you sleep with her in our bed?"

H: "Where else would we sleep?"

W: "Would you let her drive my car?"

H: "Probably, it is almost new."

W: "Would you replace my pictures with hers?"

H: "That would seem like the proper thing to do."

W: "Would you give her my jewelry?"

H: "No, I'm sure she'd want her own."

W: "Would you take her golfing with you?

H: "Yes, those are always good times."

W: "Would she use my clubs?

H: "No, she's left-handed."

W: . . . silence . . .

H: "Shit."

A husband and his wife wake up in the morning. The wife nudges her husband on the side:

—Dear, today is twenty five years since we got married.

—Yes? And, so what?

—Maybe we'll kill a fattened boar?

—And why is the boar guilty?!

A husband and his wife were sitting watching a TV program about psychology and explaining the phenomenon of "mixed emotions."

The husband turned to his wife and said:

"Honey, that's a bunch of crap. I bet you can't tell me anything that will make me happy and sad at the same time."

She said:

"Out of all your friends, you have the biggest penis . . ."

A husband comes back home from fishing—his wife meets him at the door:

—What have you caught?

—Analyses are not ready yet!

A husband is a person of repeated use.

A husband says to his wife, "I'm going to take a nap and I want you to wake me up when I want to have a drink."

"How will I know when you want a drink?"

It's easy, honey. Just wake me up!"

A man is walking down the street. A pretty young lady is going towards him. He thinks: "If my wife would have such legs . . ."

Several steps later another pretty woman is going towards him and he thinks: "If my wife would have such breasts . . ."

He comes back home and his wife opens the door for him. He says her: "My dear, you aren't going to believe it. I thought about you all the time!

An archaeologist is the best husband any woman can have; the older she gets, the more interested he is in her.

I was drunk because my wife didn't allow me to have a snack, saying: "Those who don't work—don't eat!"

An excellent family man, a devoted friend, a tireless lover . . . And all this is not me.

A smart wife never shouts at her husband.

Orders are given by a calm and clear voice.

A web-camera has been purchased for our daughter and now almost a third of her room is ideally cleaned!

A wife found her husband in bed with his mistress. She silently packed up her things and quickly left . . . and, by the way, I must say that things in the mistress's apartment were very expensive.

A wife tells her husband in a weary voice:
"I want something but I do not know with whom . . ."

Wife's orders:
"Behave decently at the table! Do not chomp and do not crackle money!"

—**D**ear, if I die, will you cry?
—Certainly, dear, you know already that I cry at each trifle.

"**D**ear son, how have you been?
Your mother and I are fine. We miss you. Please sign off your computer and come downstairs for something to eat. Love, Dad."

—**D**ear, why don't we go anywhere?
—OK, when I carry the garbage out tomorrow I will take you with me for sure.

—**D**ear, why have you never told me when you reach orgasm?
—Because you do not allow me to call you at work.

—**D**octor, my wife and I have had problems in our sexual relationship for two years.

We have five children and wish to have one more but neither my wife nor I can be excited to engage in sex.

—You know, I can give you some advice. Come back home, undress in your wife's presence, undress her as well, jump on her and start sex.

Two days later a doctor receives a phone call from his visitor:

—Doctor, thank you, everything is OK. I followed your instructions and my wife was frightened at first but then all turned out fine. But, doctor, if you only heard how our children were laughing . . .

Do not criticize your wife. Those things that you find her lacking have probably prevented her to choose a better husband.

Feeling Around . . .

A husband and a wife are in bed together. She feels his hand rubbing against her shoulder.

"Oh honey, that feels good!"—she says.

His hand moves to her breast.

"Gee, honey, that feels wonderful!"—she says.

His hand moves to her leg.

"Oh, honey, don't stop!"—she begs.

But he stops . . .

"Why did you stop?"—she cries.

"I found the remote . . ."—he replies.

He:

—A friend of mine told me that husbands sell their wives in some African countries.

She:

—And would you sell me?

He:

—No, I would make somebody a gift.

There is no more paradoxical a phrase than: "I gave him my best years!" On the one hand, a woman complains about the years she spent with "this asshole", and on the other hand she recognizes that these very years were the best in her life.

He always listens to his wife with an open mouth to balance the sound pressure inside and outside of his ear membrane.

—Hello, who're you calling for?

—Is your father home?

—No, he's out of town.

—Did he leave on vacation?

—No, he left with my mother.

The wife unexpectedly enters into the reception room of the managing director and sees that the secretary is sitting on her husband's lap. Not puzzled, her husband dictates: "On this basis I ask to allocate the second chair for my reception. And now the signature."

—Honey, I think that we should solve all problems together.

—At last! Come here and we'll solve the mathematical tasks for our son together.

—Honey, I lost two pounds.

—Do not forget to flush it, please.

—What do you call a woman whom you hate and love at the same time?
—A wife.

—What do you call a woman who knows where her husband is all the time?
—A widow.

—How do you give the more freedom to a woman?
—Increase the size of the kitchen.

A husband and his wife in bed:
—Dear, take me!
—I'm not going to go anywhere . . .

A husband communicates with his wife:
—When our neighbor replaced his furniture we also bought a new set, then he bought a TV and you made me do the same. I'm not talking about the car! But what do we do now?
—He got something new again? What is it?
—He got a new wife!

A husband to his wife:
"Tell me honestly, how long does it take for you to be ready in 15 minutes?"

—I cannot understand whether I love my husband or not.
—And why are you in doubt?
—Because I always think not of him during sex.
—And about whom do think of?
—About a man with whom I'm engaged in sex . . .

An ideal husband is always married to the other woman.

—I'd like to go out hunting with my friends if you have no objections.
—Go! I'm not going to hold you by the horns . . .

I understand nothing in a joint life with a woman!
Why the income of my wife is HER income, and MY income is OURS?

—I earn so much that I can support three women like you.
—In that case, my mother and my grandmother will live with us.

If the first marriage turned out to be a mistake . . . the second wife will pay for that.

If your husband is jealous—it means that he loves you, and if he isn't jealous—it means that he knows nothing yet.

If your wife wants to learn how to drive a car, the most important thing to do is not to stand in her way.

If you want your husband to have more money, do not take it away from him.

—I'm hot! Dear, what will the neighbours think if I show up naked in our backyard?
—You know, they'll think that I don't have enough money for your clothing.

This is my third marriage, and my husband's last one.

It's well known that a man says about 5,000 words a day, and a woman says twice as much. I don't know if that is true but my problem is when I'm back home from work my limit of words is used up already, but my wife still has plenty of words to say.

I understand that it's possible to live with one woman, but how to live with the same one?!

—I want my husband to pay more attention to me.
—Get any perfume that smells like a computer.

I would lie much less if my wife asked fewer questions.

Married couple. 10 years in marriage. Bed. There was just sex.
—Dear, have I ceased to be attractive to you?
—Have you tried to see even the most interesting movie over 2000 times?

Matrimony is a way from unforgettable sex to the not remembered one.

Mismatch is when one of the spouses hates the other and vice versa.

—My dear, we have been married for 5 years and never agree with each other.
—We have been married for 6 years.

My wife and I lived happily for 25 years . . . until our marriage.

Nothing beautifies a woman better than the absence of her husband.

—Oh, when will summer come . . . ?

—A real summer will come when you earn enough money for it . . .

She says:

—Honey, I think you love soccer more than you love me!

He says:

—Well, dear, but I love you more than hockey!

A second marriage is a victory of hope over common sense.

Take care of your wife! The next one may be even worse!

They engaged in sex so seldom that their relationships could be called casual.

To give a woman pleasure in bed, leave her alone and let her have a good sleep.

—Today—me, tomorrow—you, the day after tomorrow—Mommy . . .

—Daddy, are you sure that the family panties should be worn that way?

Trousers are more important for you than your wife because there are many places where it is possible to go without your wife.

Well, I'm not right, but you can, at least, ask me for a pardon?

—What do you think if we cheat on each other to revive our family life?

—No, it's useless, I already tried . . .

—What is the difference between a battery and a woman?
—The battery has a positive side.

What woman can be loved and hated at the same time?
-Certainly, the wife.

—Why didn't you rescue your wife when she was drowning?
—I didn't know that she was drowning. She was shouting as usual . . .

Why is it when your wife becomes pregnant all her female friends rub her tummy and say "Congratulations". But none of them rub your dick and say "Well done"?

Wife is standing on the scale:
—Oh, why am I so small!
Husband:
—Don't you wish to say—plump?
—Not at all, just what I said. According to standards a woman with my weight should be 20 centimetres higher.

Wife is talking with her husband:
—It would be better if I married the devil!
—What are you talking about, my dear! Marriages between blood relatives are forbidden!

Wife talks with her husband:
—One person came and said that he is your close relative and can prove it.
—He is, probably, a full idiot.
—Certainly. But he, probably, also has other proofs.

You got married to a Russian wife and she drank so much of your Jewish blood that she became a Jewess.

A wife is a person who helps her husband overcome the problems which he wouldn't have if he had not married her!

I wrote down my mistress's phone number under the name of «LOW BATTERY». Now, when she calls me on my cell phone and I am not there, for some reason, my wife just plugs it in to charge.

The photo of my wife in my wallet reminds me that money could be in its place.

Happy couple: he does what she wants and she does what she wants.

I had a serious talk with my husband and now he does not smoke, does not drink and does not walk . . . Currently, he quietly lies in the emergency room!

—No, I'm not fat! My brother tells me that I have a perfect figure.
—Dear, he is a mathematician, and a perfect figure for him is a ball!

—Honey, do you love me?
—Yes . . .
—But how?
—How? How strange it is!

A man with a wedding ring: "Women, be careful, I'm married!"
A woman with a wedding ring, "Men! Be brave—I'm married!"

—Masha, I beg you! Let's divorce! I have no more strength to live this way!
—No, Sasha, you married a widow, and leave me as a widow . . .

A woman has to do housework with pleasure otherwise she will still do it but without pleasure.

A happy marriage is when one spouse snores and the other does not hear.

—How do you feed your husband?
—Well, I give him the same food I cook for us.

Wife:
—Why are you so ill-mannered?! Since my mother moved in with us, you don't pay attention to her at all. You could take her out from time to time . . .
Husband:
—No sense. She always finds the way home.

Everything that woman does at home is unnoticed.
It becomes visible when she doesn't do it.

Man never has to complain about two things: his wife and his car.
He chose them himself!

The wife listens to her husband only when he talks on the phone with another woman.

A successful marriage is when there is an opportunity to have a mistress and there is no desire.

The biggest misconception by women: he is changing . . .
The biggest mistake men make: she's not going anywhere.

—Why do you want to divorce your husband?
—We have different religious views.
—And more specifically?
—He does not recognize me as a goddess!

Parenting is the process of removing your personal flaws in your children.

Taking a woman to bed:
What is the difference between girls/women aged: 8, 18, 28, 38, 48, 58, 68, and 78?
At 8—You take her to bed and tell her a story.
At 18—You tell her a story and take her to bed.
At 28—You don't need to tell her a story to take her to bed.
At 38—She tells you a story and takes you to bed.
At 48—She tells you a story to avoid going to bed.
At 58—You stay in bed to avoid her story.
At 68—If you take her to bed, that'll be a story!
At 78—What story? What bed? Who the hell are you?

Divorce:
A husband is asked:
—What is the reason for your divorce?
—We have different interests. She is interested in men, and I am interested in women.

Do not show off your wife better than anyone: women might be offended, and men will want to be sure.

A good hostess has a husband who is fed, a poor hostess has a husband who is fed up.

And now about the equality of the sexes:
I think my wife has the right to do whatever she wants. The only thing is it should be tasty.

My wife is a Russian champion at light heavyweight in boxing. I can say nothing bad about her.

Do you want to enjoy the enigmatic smile of Mona Lisa, without visiting the Louvre? Ask your wife how she uses up your salary . . .

In order to keep peace in the family you need love, patience, understanding, and two computers . . .

—When you make love do you talk with your husband?
—If he calls, why not.

Wife laments her husband:
—I was deaf and blind, when I married you!
—See, I healed you from these serious diseases!

Marriage is an event when a man stops buying flowers and begins to buy vegetables.

Husband looking for a marriage certificate in a drawer:

—Honey, where is this piece of paper on imprisonment?

—No, my dear, this is your lifetime subscription for three meals a day.

If your wife calls you by the wrong name in a dream . . . answer her and you will not regret it!

Marriage is established in order to cope with the difficulties which would never have existed without marriage.

—I want a divorce.

—For what reason?

—There are many reasons. But the most important one—I'm married!

—Who should my child should resemble?

—His father, of course . . .

—Fool! The son must be like my husband!

A new husband asks his wife on their wedding night:

—Honey, tell me frankly, am I the first man you slept with?

—Well, if you're going to sleep, then yes.

KIDS SPEAK

A dead cat is lying on the roadside.

3-years old *Vovochka* asks Mom:

—What happened to it?

—It has died and gone to the heaven.

—Oh, God. And who threw it back?

A lesson of drawing in a children's kindergarten. A teacher approaches a girl who paints something with ecstasy:

—What're you drawing?

—God.

—But, in fact, nobody knows what God looks like.

—They will, once I'm finished.

The son of my friend sits with fastened eyes.

Parents give him various objects and he guesses:

—A pencil.

—Correct.

—A ball.

—Correct.

—A machine.

—Correct.

Then his daddy gives him a sock and he is thinking long, and then says:

—A sock.

He thought a little more having smelled it and says:

—Dad's.

—**D**ad,—a teenage girl enters into her father's den says,—I'd like to kiss you good-bye before I go to school!

—You're too late, honey. Your mother just did that two minutes ago, and I don't have any cash.

—**D**addy, does Mom drive our car better than you?

—Well, I cannot tell.

—You said that it's impossible to drive on a hand brake, and here Mom has passed twelve kilometres!

—**D**addy, why do the cocks crow so early?

—Because they want to be heard. Then, when the hens wake up it'll be impossible.

—**D**addy, is it true that you should respond with good to the bad?

—Yes, son, that's true.

—Then give me some money to buy an ice-cream . . . I broke your glasses.

—**D**addy, are the words DIFFICULT, COMPLEX, and HARD synonyms?

—No, Son!

DIFFICULT—to refuse an offer to drink.

COMPLEX—to calculate the optimum dose.

HARD—it is in the morning.

Grandmother:

—Here, *Genechka*, you're already three years old. Ask Mom and Daddy if they have bought brother or sister for you.

Genya:

—What do you need spend money for? Mom is still young and she can give a birth as well.

I asked my dad where the children come from, and he said people download them from the Internet.

I'd like to assist my son with putting on his shoes. To accelerate the process I've decided to help:

—Give me your leg.

My son lifts a leg but it seems to me that this is the wrong one. I say:

—Give me another one!

He submits another. I understand that for the first time he was right:

—Give me another one!

My son surprisingly looks back, makes a helpless gesture and says:

—It's not present any more!

I got a 'D' at school today.

—Why?

—Well, in an essay "How I spent my summer" I wrote: "Thank you, it was wonderful".

In a Zoo:

—Dad, and why does this gorilla look so spitefully at me?

—Wait son, it was just the cash department.

In a kindergarten the five year old children discuss parents:
"They don't know what they want! They taught me to go and speak and now they want me to be sitting and silent?!"

Lesson in middle school:
Teacher:
—Maria, go to the map and find North America.
Maria:
—Here it is.
Teacher:
—Correct. Now class, who discovered America?
Class:
—Maria.

My son wrote a letter to Santa Claus: "Send me a sister!"
Response from Santa Claus: "Send me your mother!"

Teacher:
—*Sasha*, why are you doing your math multiplication on the floor?
Sasha:
—You told me to do it without using tables . . .

Teacher:
—*Vova*, how do you spell 'crocodile'?
Vova:
—K-R-O-K-O-D-I-A-L.
Teacher:
—No, that's wrong.
Vova:
—Maybe it is wrong, but you asked me how I spell it.

Teacher:

—David, what is the chemical formula for water?

David:

—H I J K L M N O.

Teacher:

—What are you talking about?

David:

—Yesterday you said it's H to O.

Teacher:

—*Masha*, name one important thing we have today that we didn't have ten years ago.

Masha:

—Me!

Teacher:

—*Gosha*, why do you always get so dirty?

Gosha:

—Well, I'm a lot closer to the ground than you are.

Teacher:

—Masha, give me a sentence starting with 'I'.

Masha:

—I is . . .

Teacher:

—No, Masha . . . Always say, 'I am.'

Masha:

—All right . . . 'I am the ninth letter of the alphabet.'

Teacher:

—George Washington not only chopped down his father's cherry tree, but also admitted it. Now, Louie, do you know why his father didn't punish him?

Louie:

—Because George still had the axe in his hand.

Teacher:

—Now, Simon, tell me frankly, do you say prayers before eating?

Simon:

—No sir, I don't have to, my Mom is a good cook.

Teacher:

—Michael, your composition on 'My Dog' is exactly the same as your brother's. Did you copy his?

Michael:

—No, sir. It's the same dog.

Teacher:

—*Ivan*, what do you call a person who keeps on talking when people are no longer interested in?

Ivan:

—A teacher.

Mother asks *Vovochka*:

—Why have you soiled your new pants?

—Mom, sorry, but I fell so quickly and didn't have enough time to take them off.

—Mom!—asks a nine-year old Katya,—you know that vase, that passes in our family from generation to generation?

—Yes,—answered mother,—well, and what is it then?

—So, my generation has just dropped it . . .

My name was David, but that sounded old fashioned. So I shortened it to DVD.

A ballerina rose gracefully en pointe and extended one slender leg behind her, like a dog at a fire hydrant.

My son (four years old) has heard plenty of Russian national fairy tales.

We go along the street with him and suddenly he whispers with an excited voice:

—Daddy, look, a tractor digs the Russian soil!

My son has fallen asleep on the sofa and daddy decided to shift him to bed.

He took him cautiously but the son whispers through a dream:

—Put me where I've been taken.

My son is six years old. He closely looks at the teacher's manicure.

—*Olga Aleksandrovna*, you have such a long nails . . .

—Yes. Do you like them?

—Yes, probably . . . for trees . . . to climb up well.

My son is sick. We hired a nurse, and she came the first time.

Danya (3.5 years) takes her hand and arranges an excursion around the house.

—This is the hall, this is the bedroom, this is my room, and those are my toys.

They come into the kitchen:

—Here is my cottage cheese for breakfast and flakes for lunchtime. Medicine is on the table. I eat my meal twice a day.

The nurse asks me:

—Are you sure that he needs the nurse?

Mom to her son:

—Sasha, and am I beautiful?

—Yes, you are.

—And what is beautiful?

—Your high-heeled shoes.

Schoolchildren are going home:

—*Sveta*, let me carry your bag!

—It's not heavy.

—I'm not a very strong boy!

Seva is a three years old.

We are testing his hearing at the doctor office.

The doctor whispers: "Sweet".

Seva replies: "I have an allergy and it's unacceptable for me . . ."

Six-year old Pete very much wished to have a dog, and, at last, he was presented with a huge St. Bernard. Pete is in deep thoughtfulness then passes by the enormous dog and asks me:

—Has it been presented to me or me to it?

Son asks his father:

—How was I born?

—A stork brought you.

—Daddy, there're so many beautiful girls around and you f . . . storks!

The first-grader comes home from school on September 1st and says to her parents:

—That's all, I'm not going to attend that school anymore!

—Why?

—I cannot write! I cannot read! And in addition to that they don't allow me to speak!

It has been explained to my niece where children come from. Her daddy returns from his duty and she runs towards him and shouts:

—Hooray! Hooray! Daddy's arrived! Spermatozoa have been brought!

Olga is a three year old. She sits with a toy stethoscope in her hands:

—I'm fishing!

—Olga, this is for a doctor!

—All right, I'm a doctor. And what disturbs you?

—Yes, here, my throat hurts. Can you help?

—I cannot.

—Why!?

—I'm catching fish . . .

Vovka was fighting with his girlfriend Masha in kindergarten. They have been friends since they were babies. Today I woke my son in the morning. He didn't react. I pulled off the blanket and quietly tickled his heel. Vovka whispered through a dream with a smile:

—Well, Maaashaa! . . .

—*Sasha*, is it true that monkeys are similar to people?

—True!

—And how to check it?

—Give the monkey a cigarette and a bottle of beer!

We are coming back from our friends late at night.

In view of headlights there are two maiden figures in the short skirts.

"Girls walk at night and search for adventures"—I comment.

We pass 50 meters and are come across group of guys drinking beer.

"Here adventures begin!"—my 9-year old son responds.

We are visiting our relatives. There are three small kittens in the house.

My *Alyona* (4 years), naturally, decided to patronize them, nurse them, and drag them everywhere with her. She enters the room where we are sitting and shouts:

—Dad, there's one kitten that put its face in milk and everything is going to be dirty now?

My husband says sluggishly:

—No, it should be licked up.

Alyona turns to me:

—Mom, will you lick it up?!

We have the apartment with adjacent rooms. Somehow we lay down in the evening to sleep—children are in one room, we are in another one.

I have already almost fallen asleep and suddenly I hear my daughter (3 years old) asks so loudly:

—Daddy, and Daddy, has you slept once with two women?

You can imagine my amazement.

Having found nothing to answer I say:

—No.

And she is having sighed:

—All right, I will go.

—**M**om, I was vaccinated today at school.

—Against what?

—Against my will!

—**D**ad, will you still grow up?

—No, my son.

—So why are you eating?

A teacher asks a kid:

—Why do you need ears?

—In order to see everything.

—But you have the eyes for that.

—That may be so. But if there are no ears my cap will slide over my eyes and I will see nothing.

A third grade student is asked by a teacher:

—How many letters are in the alphabet?

—Seven.

-?!

—A-L-P-H-A-B-E-T.

Vova raised his hand during the history lesson:

—*Maria Ivanovna*, my dad says that we evolved from apes. Is this true?

—*Vovochka*, do not bother me! I'm not interested in the history of your family!

—Mommy, is it true that God gives us food?

—Yes, you could say so.

—And is it true that the stork brings children?

—Yes.

—And that Santa brings presents?

—Yes, dear.

—Then, tell me, what do we need Daddy for?

"You need to eat well, dear!" the mother says to her seven-year-old daughter. "You know what happens to girls that don't . . ."

"Yes, I know," says the girl. "They become models."

A father is having a problem getting his five-year-old daughter to fall asleep. Finally, she suggests, "Daddy, why don't you just whisper something into my ear the way you do with Mommy?"

The father does just that, and the daughter falls asleep murmuring, "No, not tonight, honey, I'm so tired."

—Daddy, can you tell me, how did people finally learn that the earth is round?

—Well, son, haven't you ever seen a globe?

—Dad, why do they say that children under 14 can't watch this movie?

—Just take a seat and be quiet, son, and you will see why.

—Daddy, where do little elephants come from?

—Well . . .

—Just don't tell me the stork brings them. That bird wouldn't be able to lift a little elephant!

A teacher asks her student's mother, "Why do you send your son to this musical school to learn to play piano? He doesn't have an ear for it."

"That's not important!" the student's mother replies. "We send him here not to listen, but to play."

How many times do I have to explain to you," the teacher says, "that one half, compared to another half, cannot be smaller or bigger?! And yet the bigger half of this class doesn't understand it!"

When is your birthday, Katya?" the teacher asks her little student.

"July 21," the student answers.

"And what year?"

"Every year," the student reports.

So, *Kolya*, how do you like your new mother!" a newly remarried father asks his little son.

"You know Daddy," the replies sadly, "I think they fooled us; she doesn't look new at all!"

Why are you so wet?" a mother asks her little son.

"We played dog."

"You were the dog?"

"No, I was the tree."

Do you have any complaints about your ears or nose?" a doctor asks his little patient.

"Yes, I do, doctor. They're in the way every time I put my T-shirt on."

"Your father is going to turn gray when he sees your report card," a teacher says, handing the papers to her student.

"No, he won't", the student says.

"He doesn't care how you do at school?" the teacher asks.

'It's not that he doesn't care," the student explains. He's just bald."

—Mom, can I go to the washroom?

—Did you finish your homework?

"How did mother find out that you didn't wash your hands this time?" the father asks his son.

"I forgot to wet the soap."

"Is it true that I was born at night?" a little boy asks his mother.

"Yes, it is, honey."

I hope I didn't wake you up, Mommy."

—Mommy, can you tell me where children come from?

—It's a long story, dear.

—Please, tell me at least the beginning.

"What is that?" a little boy asks her naked mother in the sauna, pointing below her waist.

"Well," says the mother, "that's sort of a sponge."

"Father has a better one," the son concludes. "It has a handle."

Our eight-year-old son, worriedly asked, "How will we keep from getting separated?"

"We'll drive slowly so that one car can follow the other," I reassured him.

"Yeah, but what if we DO get separated?" he persisted.

"Well, then I guess we'll never see each other again," I quipped.

"Okay," he said. "I'm riding with Mom."

A teacher asked her 5th grade history class, "When was Rome built?" and called on one of the boys to answer first. "Rome was built at night." was his answer.

"At night?" asked the teacher, holding her ruler firmly in her boney-knuckled hands. "How ever did you get such an idea?"

"Well," gulped the student, hoping his answer would satisfy her, "everyone knows Rome wasn't built in a day."

Sunday school students talk about the Bible:

"The people who followed the Lord were called the 12 decibels."

"A Christian should have only one wife. This is called monotony."

"The epistles were the wives of the apostles."

"The Last Supper was eaten the next morning—cold."

"The Ten Commandments are actually only five; double spaced and written in large font."

"A new Bible edition is published every two years in order to limit reselling."

"Forbidden fruit was eaten because it wasn't cafeteria food."

"The reason Cain killed Abel; they were roommates."

"The reason why Moses and his followers walked the desert for 40 years; they didn't want to ask for directions and look like freshmen."

"He split Adam and made Eve. Adam and Eve were naked, but they weren't embarrassed because mirrors hadn't been invented yet."

"Adam and Eve disobeyed God by eating one bad apple, so they were driven from the Garden of Eden . . . . Not sure what they were driven in though, because they didn't have cars."

"Adam and Eve had a son, Cain, who hated his brother as long as he was Abel."

From student essays:

The greatest writer of the Renaissance was William Shakespeare. Shakespeare never made much money and is famous only because of his plays. He lived in Windsor with his merry wives, writing tragedies, comedies and errors. In one of Shakespeare's famous plays, Hamlet rations out his situation by relieving himself in a long soliloquy. In another, Lady Macbeth tries to convince Macbeth to kill the King by attacking his manhood. Romeo and Juliet are an example of a heroic couplet. Writing at the same time as Shakespeare was Miguel Cervantes. He wrote "Donkey Hote". The next great author was John Milton. Milton wrote "Paradise Lost." Then his wife dies and he wrote "Paradise Regained."

One of the causes of the Revolutionary Wars was the English put tacks in their tea. Also, the colonists would send their parcels through the post without stamps. Finally, the colonists won the War and no longer had to pay for taxis.

During the Renaissance America began. Christopher Columbus was a great navigator who discovered America while cursing about the Atlantic. His ships were called the Nina, the Pinta, and the Santa Fe. Later the Pilgrims crossed the Ocean, and this was known as Pilgrim's Progress. When they landed at Plymouth Rock, they were greeted by Indians, who came down the hill rolling their war hoops before them. The Indian squabs carried porpoises on their back. Many of the Indian heroes were killed, along with their cabooses, which proved very fatal to them. The winter of 1620 was a hard one for the settlers. Many people died and many babies were born. Captain John Smith was responsible for all this.

Meanwhile in Europe, the enlightenment was a reasonable time. Voltare invented electricity and also wrote a book called "Candy". Gravity was invented by Issac Walton. It is chiefly noticeable in the Autumn, when the apples are falling off the trees.

Bach was the most famous composer in the world, and so was Handel. Handel was half German, half Italian and half English. He was very large. Bach died from 1750 to the present. Beethoven wrote music even though he was deaf. He was so deaf he wrote loud music. He took long walks in the forest even when everyone was calling for him. Beethoven expired in 1827 and later died for this.

France was in a very serious state. The French Revolution was accomplished before it happened. The Marseillaise was the theme song of the French Revolution, and it catapulted into Napoleon. During the Napoleonic Wars, the crowned heads of Europe were trembling in their shoes. Then the Spanish gorillas came down from the hills and nipped at Napoleon's flanks. Napoleon became ill with bladder problems and was very tense and unrestrained. He wanted an heir to inherit his power, but since Josephine was a baroness, she couldn't bear any children.

The nineteenth century was a time of many great inventions and thoughts. The invention of the steamboat caused a network of rivers to spring up. Cyrus McCormick invented the McCormick Raper, which did the work of a hundred men. Samuel Morse invented a code for telepathy. Louis Pastuer discovered a cure for rabbis. Charles Darwin was a naturalist who wrote the "Organ of the Species". Madman Curie discovered radium. And Karl Marx became one of the Marx Brothers.

Another story was William Tell, who shot an arrow through an apple while standing on his son's head.

"I'll give you my two pennies for that tomato," said the boy pointing to a beautiful, large, ripe fruit hanging on the vine.

"No," said the farmer, "I get a dime for a tomato like that one."

The small boy pointed to a smaller green one, "Will you take two pennies for that one?"

"Yes," replied the farmer, "I'll give you that one for two cents."

"OK," said the lad, sealing the deal by putting the coins in the farmer's hand, "I'll pick it up in about a week."

The things kids say . . .

"Close the curtains," requested our 2 year old granddaughter, sitting in a pool of bright light. "The sun's looking at me too hard."

My friend asked our grandson when he would turn 6. He replied, "When I'm tired of being 5."

Seeing her first hailstorm, my daughter exclaimed, "Mommy, it's raining dumplings!"

As I frantically waved away a pesky fly with a white dish towel, my granddaughter observed, "Maybe he thinks you're surrendering."

Announcing to my daughter Lori that her aunt just had a baby and it looked like her uncle, she said, "You mean he has a moustache?"

When I asked our grandson if he could name the capital of Florida, he fired right back, "capital F!"

While shampooing our son (4), I noted that his hair was growing so fast he'd soon need it cut. He replied, "Maybe we shouldn't water it so much."

My daughter told her 5-year-old friend that their van was going to be fixed. Instantly, the small fry assumed, "Oh, it's going to the tire-o-practor?"

Impressed by her 5-year-old's vocabulary, my friend complimented the young scholar, who nonchalantly responded, "I have words in my head I haven't even used yet."

The mom informed her son that she was going outside to get a little sun. "But Mommy, he gulped, "You already have a son—me!"

When our son asked about two look-alike classmates at school, we told him they were probably twins. The next day, he came home from school all bubbly and said, "Guess what? They are not only twins, they're brothers!"

The children had all been photographed and the teacher was trying to persuade them each to buy a copy of the group picture. "Just think how nice it will be to look at it when you are all grown up and say, 'There's Sasha, she's a lawyer,' or 'That's Michael, he's a doctor.'"
A small voice from the back of the room rang out, "And there's the teacher; she's still old, nasty, and wrinkled".

For weeks a six-year old lad kept telling his first-grade teacher about the baby brother or sister that was expected at his house.

One day the mother allowed the boy to feel the movements of the unborn child. The six-year old was obviously impressed, but made no comment. Furthermore, he stopped telling his teacher about the impending event.

The teacher finally sat the boy on her lap and said, "Peter, whatever has become of that baby brother or sister you were expecting at home?"

Peter burst into tears and confessed, "I think Mommy ate it!"

Murphy's Law of Children:

The later you stay up, the earlier your child will wake up the next morning.

For a child to become clean, something else must become dirty.

Toys multiply to fill any space available.

The longer it takes you to make a meal, the less your child will like it.

Yours is always the only child who doesn't behave.

If the shoe fits—it's expensive.

The surest way to get something done is to tell a child not to do it.

The gooier the food, the more likely it is to end up on the carpet.

Backing the car out of the driveway causes your child to have to go to the bathroom.

The more challenging the child, the more rewarding it is to be a parent—sometimes.

My grandson was visiting one day when he asked, "Grandma, do you know how you and God are alike?" I mentally polished my halo and I said, "No, how are we alike?" "You're both old," he replied.

When my grandson asked me how old I was, I teasingly replied, "I'm not sure." "Look in your underwear, Grandpa," he advised, "mine says I'm 4 to 6."

"Give me a sentence about a public servant," said the teacher. The small boy wrote: "The fireman came down the ladder pregnant." The teacher took the lad aside to correct him. "Don't you know what pregnant means?" she asked. "Sure," said the young boy confidently. 'It means carrying a child."

A grandfather was delivering his grandchildren to their home one day when a fire truck zoomed past. Sitting in the front seat of the fire truck was a Dalmatian dog. The children started discussing the dog's duties. "They use him to keep crowds back," said one child. "No," said another. "He's just for good luck." A third child brought the argument to a close. "They use the dogs," she said firmly, "to find the fire hydrants."

A teacher in the back country presented her students with the first half of a well-known proverb and asked them to come up with the other half. The results reveal a little of their world and their home life—remember, though, they're six-year-olds.

- Don't change horses . . . . until they stop running
- Strike while the . . . . bug is close
- It's always darkest before . . . . daylight saving time
- Never underestimate the power of . . . . termites

- You can lead a horse to water but . . . . how?
- Don't bite the hand that . . . . looks dirty
- No news is . . . . impossible
- A miss is as good as a . . . . mister
- You can't teach an old dog new . . . . math
- If you lie down with dogs, you'll . . . . stink in the morning
- Love all, trust . . . . me
- The pen is mightier than the . . . . pigs
- An idle mind is . . . . the best way to relax
- Where there's smoke there's pollution.
- Happy the bride who gets all the presents.
- A penny saved is not much.
- Two's company, three's the Musketeers.
- Don't put off till tomorrow what you put on to go to bed.
- Laugh and the whole world laughs with you, cry and you have to blow your nose.
- There are none as blind as Stevie Wonder.
- Children should be seen and not spanked or grounded.
- If at first you don't succeed get new batteries.
- When the blind lead the blind get out of the way.
- A bird in the hand is going to poop on you.

And best of all:

- 14. Better late than . . . . pregnant

A 5th grader asked her mother the age-old question, 'How did I get here?'

Her mother told her, 'God sent you.'

'Did God send you, too?' asked the child

'Yes, Dear,' the mother replied.

'What about Grandma and Grandpa?' the child persisted.

'He sent them also,' the mother said.

'Did he send their parents, too?' asked the child.

'Yes, Dear, He did,' said the mother patiently.

'So you're telling me that there has been NO sex in this family for 200 years?

No wonder everyone's so damn grouchy around here.'

Son (age 3) was watching his Mom breast-feeding his new baby sister. After a while he asked:

"Mom why have you got two? Is one for hot and one for cold milk?"

—Dad, and who do you wanted a boy or a girl?
—Generally, I just wanted your mom!

Little *Natasha* was in the garden filling a hole when I peered over the fence. Interested in what the cheeky-faced youngster was up to, I politely asked, "What are you doing there, *Natasha*?"

"My goldfish died", replied *Natasha* tearfully without looking up, "and I've just buried him."

I was very concerned of course. "That's an awfully big hole for a Goldfish, isn't it," I asked.

Natasha patted down the last heap of dirt, then replied, "That's because it is inside your fuckin' cat."

Pete (age 3) was watching his Mom breast-feeding his new baby sister. After a while he asked: "Mum why have you got two? Is one for hot and one for cold milk?"

Masha (age 5) asked her Granny how old she was. Granny replied she was so old she didn't remember any more. Melanie said, "If you don't remember you must look in the back of your panties. Mine say five to six."

Sergey (age 3) hugged and kissed his Mom good night "I love you so much that when you die I'm going to bury you outside my bedroom window."

Natasha (age 4) had an earache and wanted a pain killer. She tried in vain to take the lid off the bottle. Seeing her frustration, her Mum explained it was a child-proof cap and she'd have to open it for her. Eyes wide with wonder, the little girl asked: "How does it know it's me?"

Vera (age 4) was drinking juice when she got the hiccups. "Please don't give me this juice again," she said, "It makes my teeth cough."

Dmitry (age 4) stepped onto the bathroom scale and asked: "How much do I cost?"

Marc (age 4) was engrossed in a young couple that were hugging and kissing in a restaurant. Without taking his eyes off them, he asked his dad: "Why is he whispering in her mouth?"

Boris (age 5) was in his bedroom looking worried. When his Mom asked what was troubling him, he replied, "I don't know what'll happen with this bed when I get married. How will my wife fit in?"
Ivan (age 4) was listening to a Bible story. His dad read: "The man named Lot was warned to take his wife and flee out of the city but his wife looked back and was turned to salt." Concerned, Ivan asked: "What happened to the flea?"

Tanya (age 4) was with her mother when they met an elderly, rather wrinkled woman her Mom knew. Tanya looked at her for a while and then asked, "Why doesn't your skin fit your face?"

I think this Mom will never forget . . . . this particular Sunday sermon . . . "Dear Lord," the minister began, with arms extended toward heaven and a rapturous look on his up turned face. "Without you, we are but dust . . ." He would have continued but at that moment my very obedient daughter who was listening leaned over to me and asked quite audibly in her shrill little four year old girl voice, "Mom, what is butt dust?"

MEDICAL HUMOR

—Doctor, am I healthy?
—An autopsy will show.

—Doctor, you have to help me. I'm working like a horse, eating like a pig, and I'm tired as a dog!
—I'm afraid I can't help—I'm not a veterinarian.

—Doctor, is it true that I can improve my eyesight by eating carrots?
—Yes, it is. Have you ever seen a rabbit wearing glasses?

"Do you drink, sir?" a doctor asks his patient.
"I wouldn't mind!" the patient replies.

A man walks into a doctor's office and the doctor says to him:
—Sir, I can see you need a good pair of glasses.
—How do you know that, doctor? I just walked in!
—I'm a gynecologist.

—Hello, did you phone the ambulance?
—Yes.
—Come outside! We are here!

—

Do you suffer from erotic dreams?

—No, doctor, I enjoy them . . .

Unsuccessful surgery is a half of successful autopsy.

Grandmother comes to the drugstore:

—Do you carry iodide potassium?

—No. We've got potassium cyanide.

—And what is the difference?

—It costs two kopecks more.

Announcement:

"Good surgeon will help bad dancer".

—Well, your pulse is normal,—a doctor says.

—Doctor, take my left hand—the right is an artificial limb.

Doctor to his patient:

—We cannot amputate everything, unfortunately. Something should be treated . . .

—Doctor, my wife stutters.

—Always?

—No, only when she speaks!

—I'm afraid, sir, I cannot do anything to help you—your wife's disease is hereditary.

—Well, then send a bill for the visit to my father-in-law.

—Doctor, there's something wrong with me. I'm just forty years old but when I look in the mirror . . . Bald, bags under the eyes, wrinkles, cheeks hang, just a few teeth left. What is wrong?

—Well, I cannot exactly say, but maybe it isn't so bad? At least, you have good vision.

A man comes to a psychiatrist:

—My wife has an obsession; she thinks that someone tries to steal her dresses.

—Are you sure?

—Absolutely. She employed a special person who protects them. I found him yesterday in the closet . . .

—How do you feel?—a doctor asks a patient.

—Much better, doctor. I think that I was helped by your medicine. I most carefully followed the instructions written on the package.

—And what was written there?

—"Hold densely closed".

Drugstore:

—Do you have medicine for gonorrhea?

—Yes, please pay here.

—Please wrap it beautifully, it is going to be a gift!

A psychoanalyst to a patient:

—After your examination I have two pieces of news for you—good and bad. The bad—no doubt that you are a latent homosexual.

The patient:

—And what is good?!

The doctor sits down next to the patient:

—You are nice!

There is a test for new medicine. Patients are divided in two controlled groups. One of the patients comes to doctor:

—Doctor, why did you change my medication?

The doctor (very cautiously):

—And what forces you to think, that I have replaced it?

—You know, earlier, when I threw these tablets into a toilet bowl, they floated, and now they sink for some reason.

Two nurses talk in a maternity home:

—Who is crying so loudly? Is it the triplet that was born today at night?

—No, it is their father in the hallway.

For reasons of medical ethics, the diagnosis "Dead" for a patient was changed to "No further treatment is needed."

"The conclusion about death which I have given to you must be rewritten"—appealed the nurse manager of the surgical department at the city hospital.

"What's wrong?" she asked.

"A little misunderstanding"—the doctor replied, took her aside and whispered:

"I signed it in a hurry, and accidentally wrote my name and title under "Cause of Death."

A pregnant woman and her husband asked a doctor whether they can have sex during her pregnancy.

He told them that in the first trimester they can do it the normal style. During the second trimester they should do it in a doggy stile, and in the third trimester they should be limited by the wolf style.

"Wolf style?"—asked the husband—"what is that?"

"This is when you're lying near your wife and howl!"

"Patients awaiting reception, please, do not share with each other the symptoms of your illnesses! It impedes diagnosis".

A psychiatrist with 15 years of experience says:

"Healthy people do not exist, there exist only the unexamined!"

"Take your clothes off, please"—says the doctor to a girl.

"Why? I have a sore ear!"

"I am an eye doctor, you should visit an otolaryngologist."

The possibilities of medicine are endless. Limited is the capacity of patients.

Doctor, since I got married, something is wrong with my eyes! I DO NOT SEE MONEY!

Medicine is the highest art to draw conclusions about the symptoms of a disease on the basis of the causes of death.

Doctor, I ate pizza along with the packaging. Am I going to die?

—Well, everyone will die someday.

—All will die? God, what have I done?

A man enters a doctor's office, his hands are trembling.

—Do you drink a lot?—asks the doctor.

—Not really . . . I slop out a lot!

Failed surgery is already a half of successful autopsy.

Doctor's recommendations of how to take the prescribed pills:

"Take these two pills at night and take another two tablets in the morning if you wake up . . .

—Doctor, will my temperature go down?

—Of course. It will be close to the room temperature by the evening.

World Symposium of Proctologists is opened by the famous academic with these words:

—Gentlemen! It is a great honor to open the World Symposium of Proctologists! Excuse me that I turned to you with my face!

—The doctor said that I have multiple sclerosis, rheumatism, asthma, angina . . .

—Enough, enough! Better tell me what you do not have.

—My teeth.

A doctor to a patient:

—Take it easy! Your head wound was quite heavy, but the main thing, we were able to avoid an amputation . . .

Doctor *Ivanov* has a rare hobby. He collects the last words of his patients . . .

A phone call to an emergency room:
—Tell me, is *Ivanov* still alive?
—Not yet.

Hello, free doctor!
Welcome, terminally ill patient!

After an examination of the patient, doctor approaches his wife.
—You know, madam, I really do not like the looks of your husband—he says delicately.
The woman nods knowingly:
—Doctor, I do not like him either, but he is very loved by my children!

—**A**nd now, dear patient, bend the knee.
—Well, and in what direction?

—**D**octor, every day I go to the store for some vodka. Tell me, am I a shopaholic?

Sclerosis cannot be cured, but can be forgotten.

What else should I eat to lose weight?

Patient-millionaire to his doctor:
—You know, I decided not to pay you the fee, but instead I'll put you in my will. Are you satisfied?
—Yes, of course. Just give me back my prescription, and I will make some changes to it.

Dentist:

—That's it, here's your tooth!

Patient:

—Thank you, doctor, here's an armrest from your chair . . .

Psychiatrist:

—It is difficult to diagnose. Perhaps this is alcoholism?

Patient:

—Well, doctor! I'll be back when you're sober.

The possibilities of medicine are endless. The capabilities of patients are limited.

It doesn't matter how much vodka you drink—your body still consists of 65% water!

Only treatment can be more expensive than health.

—**W**here are you taking me?" the patient, lying in a hospital bed, asks the nurses who are pushing his bed down the hallway.

—To the morgue.

—But I'm not dead yet!

—Well, we have not reached of, yet . . .

—**D**octor, my wife stutters.

—Always?

—No, only when she speaks!

At the doctor's office:

—Tell me, how do you go to sleep?

—I count to three and go to sleep.

—What, only to three?

—Well, sometimes up to half past three.

A patient went to a doctor. Patient was suffering from insomnia, nervous breakdown and Depression.

After some checking the doctor said,

"This medicine is for insomnia, this one is for nervous break-down, and also take this one for depression.

Patient: "Thank you very much, doctor, but do you have any other medicine besides vodka?"

MILITARY JOKES

A bomb always lands in the center of an explosion.

—An atom consists of a nucleus and electrons flying around it.
—So, what's between the nucleus and electrons?
—Nothing, just air . . .

A top secret document: "Burn before reading."

Two major army rules:
    #1. The commanding officer is always right.
    #2. If the commanding officer is not right, see rule #1.

General Augereau visited a newly appointed general Bonaparte and saw him jumping trying to get his hat from a high hammered nail.
"Let me help you, Sir",—said Augereau. "I'm taller than you by a head."
"You aren't taller",—responded Bonaparte, "You are longer! But I can deprive you of this advantage".

I don't know how it's supposed to be but you are doing it wrong!

—

—In case of nuclear attack, put on a white bag and SLOWLY proceed to the nearest cemetery.
—Why slowly?
—So you won't create a panic!

Comrade Cadet, don't make that smart face! Don't forget that you are here to become an officer!

Let's say we have *m* number of tanks. No, that's not enough—let's say we have *n* number of tanks.

Private *Ivanov*. Dig a trench from this fence to lunchtime!

Reduce the term of military service for a maximum of 9 months!
This allows fathers to return to children at the right moment.

Sign on the roof of the building:
"Greetings to participants of the defense of the city of *Kharkov*, FROM the fascist aggressors".

The commanding officer at the Russian military academy (the equivalent of a 4-star general in the U.S.) gave a lecture on Potential Problems and Military Strategy. At the end of the lecture, he asked if there were any questions.
An officer stood up and asked, "Will there be a third world war? And will Russia take part in it?" The general answered both questions in the affirmative.
Another officer asked, "Who will be the enemy?"
The general replied, "All indications point to China."

Everyone in the audience was shocked. A third officer remarked, "General, we are a nation of only 150 million, compared to the 1.5 billion Chinese. Can we win at all, or even survive?"

The general answered, "Just think about this for a moment. In modern warfare, it is not the quantity of soldiers that matters but the quality of an army's capabilities. For example, in the Middle East we have had a few wars recently where 5 million Jews fought against 150 million Arabs, and Israel was always victorious."

After a small pause, yet another officer—from the back of the auditorium asked, "Do we have enough Jews?"

—Cadet *Sidorov*, of what material is a shutter made of?

—From a blued steel, comrade, the ensign!

—Correct. And of what material is a firing-pin made of?

—From a blued steel, comrade, the ensign!

—Incorrect. You badly studied the textbook. It is clearly written: "From the same material."

—What is the most destructive weapon in the world?

—The Aurora's gun*. One shot . . . and about seventy five years of disaster . . .

*ship's gun that gave the start signal to the Russian Bolshevik Revolution of 1917

When they capture you they'll beat you up and torture you but you won't say anything . . . Not because you are so strong but because you know nothing!

Why do you wear the pants made by the most probable adversary?

"You! There! Listen here!"

—Lieutenant, you are coward and scoundrel! I challenge you to a duel!
—And I'll not come!
—Why not?
—Because I'm coward and scoundrel!

Sergeant asks a soldier:
—Did you take something from mosquitoes?
—Yes! I took from mosquitoes all the best qualities: agility, courage and resistance!

"Humans always make mistakes",—a commander began talking with a sapper's wife.

A paratrooper can reach speeds up to 280 km/h, if he does not open his parachute.
Only a sapper can develop a greater speed.

"Do you know who I am, soldier?" an angry general demands from a soldier, who had failed to salute him in a busy shopping mall on his way out.
"Hey guys!" the soldier says to his friends ". Look! This old fart doesn't know who he is!"

Recruiting officer: "Where would you like to serve, young man?"
Draftee: "At the General Staff, comrade major!"
Recruiting officer: "Are you crazy?"
Draftee: "Is that mandatory?"

A soldier on kitchen duty is ordered to peel potatoes:
"I thought the army would have a machine to do this nowadays," he complained.
It does," the sergeant replies, "and you're its latest model."

—You could be a sergeant if you didn't drink, private!
—Sergeant?! When I'm drunk, I feel like a general!

—Did you lose your arm in combat?
—No, on my way to the draft office.

A sergeant explains the basics of ballistics to a group of recruits:
"The bullet's path is a curve called a parabola and it looks like this . . ."
"Comrade Sergeant," one soldier raises his hand. "But that means that, if we hold a gun on its side, we can shoot from behind the corner, doesn't it?"
The sergeant is visibly puzzled by this question. He scratches his head and snaps, "It does, I suppose! But a Soviet soldier would never shoot from behind a corner!"

Top secret documents must be destroyed before they are read.

A recruit examines the food that's been served to him in the garrison dining room:
"Do I have any choice here? He asks his sergeant.
"Yes, you do," the sergeant replies. "You may eat it, or not."

Politics, Economy

According to the rules of politic correctness the implacable enemies became the implacable friends.

A democratic country differs from a totalitarian one because shadowing citizens, prosecution of heterodoxy, juggling of election results, closing of oppositional mass media, tortures in prisons, and political murders in a democratic country is carried out exclusively in a democratic way.

"If your government is big enough to give you everything you want, it is big enough to take away everything you have."—Thomas Jefferson

All local wars pursue local aims. The purpose of world war is peace.

A national culture begins not with canonization and sacred reverence but from the water drain and clearing of waste.

—And what do you have in the *Kremlin*?
—Well . . . *Tsar-Bell*! But it doesn't ring!
—And what else?
—*Tsar-Gun*! It doesn't shoot!

—Ha! And what else?

—And *Duma* . . .

A plumber, *Ivanov*, was called to fix a faucet. It was a gasket problem but he said that the SYSTEM should be changed . . . He was arrested and became a political prisoner.

Authorities live on taxing people, and the authority's representatives—on taking bribes.

Democracy, as it is known, does not know subjunctive.

Democracy is a political system in which the elections are conducted and the democrats always win the elections.

Democracy is the same as bureaucracy . . . only a DEMO.

Democracy is two wolves and a lamb voting on what to have for lunch. Liberty is a well-armed lamb contesting the vote.

Democracy is when everyone does what a main democrat orders.

The dollar is up today and instantly down again. That reminds me of my own intimate organ.

—Do you have an invitation to Putin's inauguration?

—Oh, I have a membership.

Due to the crisis a method of medical starvation became very popular.

Every husband is dissatisfied with how his wife and the government spend money. The only difference is that he is not afraid to abuse the government openly.

A free system does not allow a slacker and a worker to be equal.

Gazprom and Ukraine signed a contract—gas has gone to Ukraine and to Europe. Ukrainian newspapers came out with the headlines:
"Those damn Russians have again spoiled the fresh air in Ukraine".

George Bush, Queen Elizabeth, and Vladimir Putin all die and go to hell. While there, they spot a red phone and ask what the phone is for. The devil tells them it is for calling back to Earth.
Putin asks to call Russia and talks for 5 minutes. When he is finished the devil informs him that the cost is a million roubles, so Putin writes him a check.
Next Queen Elizabeth calls England and talks for 30 minutes. When she is finished the devil informs her that the cost is 6 million pounds, so she writes him a check.
Finally George Bush gets his turn and talks for 4 hours. When he is finished the devil informs him that the cost is $5.00.
When Putin hears this he gets angry and asks the devil why Bush's phone call to the USA is so cheap.
The devil smiles and replies: "Since Obama took over the country it has gone to hell so it's a local call."

Have you understood all this correctly . . . ?
If you cross the Afghan border illegally you get shot.
If you cross the Chinese border illegally you may never be heard from again.

If you cross the Cuban border illegally you will be thrown into political prison to rot.

If you cross the Iranian border illegally you are detained indefinitely.

If you cross the North Korean border illegally you get twelve (12) years hard labor.

If you cross the Saudi Arabian border illegally you will be jailed.

If you cross the Venezuelan border illegally you will be branded a spy and your fate will be sealed.

If you cross the U.S. border illegally you get:

— a job
— a driver's license
— Social Security card
— Welfare
— food stamps
— credit cards
— subsidized rent or a loan to buy a house
— free education
— free health care
— millions of dollars to publish documents in your native language
— the right to participate in protest demonstrations related to restraints of your rights
— a lobbyist in Washington
— in many instances you can vote.

Advanced technologies have not been and are not present in Russia. Lemons do not grow in the North Pole.

—What is a person who doesn't distinguish between colors called?

—A color-blind person.

—And whatis a person who distinguishes between colors called?

—A racist.

If a diplomat says "Yes"—it actually means "It can be".
If a diplomat says "It can be"—it means "It is not present".
If a diplomat says "It is not present"—he is not a diplomat any longer.

If Americans are stupid, what can be said about those who unsuccessfully tried to overtake and surpass them for decades?

If the Health Care Reform Plan is so great why does it exempt you, Mr. President, your wife Michelle Obama, congress, senators and their families?

If the president of the USA kills a fly—a dairy crisis bursts, there is a falsification of elections in Iran, a corking of gas in Ukraine, and crowds of soldiers flee from Georgia.
This is what a globalization is all about.

If they promise a brilliant future it is time to start to put off until tomorrow.

"If you haven't had a previous conviction, it's not your merit, it's our overlook".

—Felix Dzerzhinsky

If you think that nobody cares that you're alive or not—try to miss a couple of payments to creditors.

I lied? No, I just promised change . . . I'll just change the promise!

In addition to fools and poor roads, Russia has another ailment: fools giving directions at crossroads.

"In my old age I have come to the conclusion that one useless man is a shame, two is a law firm and three or more is a Congress."

—John Adams

In order to be the best president, it is not necessary to be a good president.

Instructions for militiamen:
"Due to lack of money do not take the criminals red-handed—take them with cash".
"Due to lack of ammunition do not fire the warning shots in the air".

—Is it possible to build socialism in one single country?
—It's possible but it's better to live in another country.

"Is it true that, among all countries, the United States has the largest number of automobiles?"
"Yes, but the USSR has the most parking spaces."

It is possible to become president but it is much more complex to be a good president.

It's allowed to turn to the queen back in Great Britain. In response the Britain gays demand that they were allowed to turn their backs to prince.

It's interesting how much D. Medvedev pays V. Putin for the rent of his office.

It's not true that there are only dishonorable people in the government. Let's be objective. There are incompetent people there as well.

America has come a long way . . . from the hut of Uncle Tom to the barrack of Obama!

Look how the material well-being of the people grows:
The Russian missiles are the most winged, and the bombs—the most hydrogenous.

Mikhail Gorbachev won the Nobel Peace Prize for the collapse of the Soviet Union.
The Nobel committee with great hope presented the Nobel Peace Prize to Barrack Obama.

Monarchy—the type of government in which the highest office in the country is sexually transmitted.

Money comes and goes but the need for it remains.

The naked truth is politically incorrect.

Obama killed a fly during an interview and the journalists made an elephant of that story.

On the eve of Israel's Independence Day someone wrote a message on the fence of the Israeli Consulate in Manila (Philippines):
"Happy birthday, Israel! You are 64 and everyone still wants to fuck you!"

"People are not only a luxury but the means of enrichment".

—Government

Politicians say that they think about the ordinary people but what they think is not specified.

Presidents are not born—presidents die.

The president is called to watch order in the country. Disorders are not interesting for him.

The problem of the Russian investigatory bodies: A trial is conducted by amateurs, and crimes are committed by professionals.

Remember that the government cannot give anything to anyone until they first take it away from someone else.

Russia first came out of the current economic crisis to enter into the next.

Russia makes the impression of great power . . . And it makes nothing more.

The American says: "I can go outside and shout: "Down with Reagan!"
And nobody will condemn or pursue me for that."
Russian *muzhik* (man) says: "I can go outside and also shout:
"Down with Reagan!"
And nobody will punish or arrest me for that!"

Some countries have oil and the rest of the world has exhaust gas.

The dream of our state is when healthy and wealthy citizen who always paid taxes, died on the day of his retirement.

The government seriously worries about our well-being. It has nothing to worry about in terms of the government well-being.

The majority of us dream about having a lot of money and to not work. 50 % of the dream has come true for many people (thanks to the economic crisis) but, alas, it's not the first 50 % of the dream.

The modern Robin Hoods take credit from banks and hand it over to the homeless.

There are only two great holidays in Russia: New Year and New Authority.

The Russian eagle is a double-headed eagle because one part of the officials sells the national wealth of the country to the developed Western countries, and another part—to the underdeveloped countries of the East.

The Russian economy depends on how cold it is in Europe.

The United States is the hospital attendant of the world—it attacks the weak and sick countries . . .

There exist three law systems:
In the American system, everything is allowed except that which is not allowed.
In the Russian system, everything is allowed even that is not allowed.

In the Byelorussian system, nothing is allowed even that is allowed.

There is political upheaval in Zimbabwe! The prime minister has eaten the president.

They had the freedom of speech. But they did not have the freedom AFTER the speech.
[It is about the ordinary people in the former Soviet Union]

Those who make peaceful revolution impossible will make violent revolution inevitable.

Two Crocodiles were sitting by the side of the lake . . .
The smaller one turned to the bigger one and said, "I can't understand how you can be so much bigger than me. We're the same age. We were the same size as kids. I just don't get it."
"Well," said the big Croc, "What have you been eating?"
"Politicians, same as you," replied the small Croc.
"Hmm . . . Well, where do you catch them?"
"Down the other side of the swamp near the parking lot by the Parliament Buildings."
"Same here. Hmm. How do you catch them?"
"Well, I crawl up under one of their Lexus cars and wait for one to unlock the car door. Then I jump out, grab them by the leg, shake the shit out of them and eat 'em!"
"Ah!" says the big Crocodile, "I think I see your problem. You're not getting any real nourishment. See, by the time you finish shaking the shit out of a Politician, There's nothing left but an asshole and a briefcase."

Two variants of the succession of events are now possible in Russia: the WORST and the UNLIKELY.

We have enjoyed so much freedom for so long that we are perhaps in danger of forgetting how much our freedom cost.

—What are your forecasts concerning a dollar exchange rate?
—A dollar will be . . . Yes, almost for certain, a dollar will be.

—What is the difference between capitalism and socialism?
—Under capitalism, one man exploits another man; under socialism, it's vice versa.

—What is the similarity between God and Barrack Obama?
—Both of them don't have a birth certificate.
—And what's the difference between them?
—God does not consider Himself Barrack Obama, and Barrack Obama considers himself God.

—What is a Soviet duet?
—It's a Soviet quartet after a performance abroad.

What is well organized in Russia is a criminality.

—What was the most luxurious nursing home in the world?
—Kremlin . . .

—Why do KGB agents work as a team of three?
—One is able to read, the other—to write, and the third one should keep an eye on these two intellectuals.

—Why has the president of Lithuania never personally met the former president of Russia?

—Because personal contacts of the KGB agents and the agents of the CIA are forbidden.

With all current Middle East politics going nowhere, we need some fresh ideas. Here is one out of the box strategy:

Israel should give some land to the Palestinians; in return the US should give Israel the entire State of Florida. Everyone will benefit from this: with all Israelis buying second homes, real estate in Florida will finally get out of limbo, triggering broad economic recovery in the US. Israel, now in close proximity to Washington, will become a major force in the Health Care overhaul and help the US regain its world leadership in high tech.

You cannot correct stupid people but you can vote for them!

Khrushchev visited a pig farm and was photographed there. In the newspaper's office, a discussion was under way about what should be the caption under the picture.

"Comrade Khrushchev among pigs,"

"Comrade Khrushchev and pigs,"

"Pigs around comrade Khrushchev,"—all was rejected.

Finally the editor makes the decision.

The caption is "The third from the left—comrade Khrushchev."

Khrushchev reduced the size of apartments, but could not make ceiling and floor joined.

He built a toilet into bathroom but could not connect plumbing and sewage system.

Five precepts of the Soviet intellectuals:

1. Don't think.
2. If you think, then don't speak.
3. If you think and speak, then don't write.
4. If you think, speak and write, then don't sign.
5. If you think, speak, write and sign, then don't be surprised.

Seven miracles of socialism

1. everyone had a job
2. in spite of the fact that everyone had a job nobody worked
3. in spite of the fact that nobody worked the plan was executed by 100%
4. in spite of the fact that plan was executed by 100%, there was nothing in the shops
5. in spite of the fact that there was nothing in the shops, everyone was provided with everything
6. in spite of the fact that everyone was provided with everything, everyone stole
7. in spite of the fact that everyone stole, as a whole all were satisfied

Six paradoxes of the socialist state:

Nobody works, but the plan is always fulfilled.

The plan is fulfilled, but the shelves in the stores are empty.

The shelves are empty, but nobody starves.

Nobody starves, but everybody is unhappy.

Everybody is unhappy, but nobody complains.

Nobody complains, but the jails are full.

People want an honest, kind, wise and strong-willed person to rule them. But the Constitution says that only one person can govern the country.

"Socialism only works in two places: Heaven where they don't need it and hell where they already have it."

—Ronald Reagan

"Politics is not a bad profession. If you succeed, there are many rewards; if you disgrace yourself, you can always write a book."

—Ronald Reagan

"It has been said that politics is the second oldest profession. I have learned that it bears a striking resemblance to the first."

—Ronald Reagan

Russia is the only country where fences are made of boards and furniture is made from sawdust.

Only in Russia you find a stripper with two college degrees and one of them is a teacher's.

In order the cows to eat less and give more milk, they should be fed less and milked more.

After a long search, what orientation to choose, the West or the East, Russia chose 'nontraditiona' orientation . . .

The government is working well.
People live poorly because they do not work in the government.

The last generation of Soviet people could not live under communism. But their children . . .

Poor children!

Democracy with elements of dictatorship is the same as constipation with elements of diarrhea.

—Can socialism be built in one country?

—It is possible to build socialism in one country, but then you have to live in another country.

According to the rules of political correctness the implacable enemies become the implacable friends.

Searching for some hot material in support of his report on the meager living conditions of ordinary Russians, a foreign journalist walks into a local bar favored by working-class folk. He approaches the drunkest visitor and politely asks for an interview.

"Go ahead!" the drunk says.

"In my country every family has a car," the journalist begins, "What about you? Do you have a car?"

"Ye-e-s-s? I do," the drunk says proudly. "In fact, I might have not one car, but two!"

"It's not possible. How could it be?"

"Well, say I hit you with this mug right now. (Hic.) They will send one car for me and another one for you in no time."

"They say the President has a great many supporters."

"That isn't true. He can still walk by himself."

Q: What is the exchange rate between a ruble, a dollar, and a pound?
A: One pound of rubles equals one dollar.

One of the Israeli generals asked if he forgives a terrorist.
He replied: "God will forgive. Our task is to arrange their meeting."

At the meeting Tony Blair to annoy Putin, said:
—And today I had a dream that I was appointed president of the Earth!
Bush assented:
—And I dreamed that I was appointed President of the Universe!
Putin takes a sip of coffee slowly and calmly responds:
—And I dreamed that I did not approve your assignments.

—When the final phase of socialism, namely communism, is built, will there still be thefts and pilfering?
—No, because everything will be already pilfered during socialism.

—What is the most permanent feature of our socialist economy?
—Temporary shortages.

—What is the difference between capitalism and socialism?
—In a capitalist society man exploits man, and in a socialist one, the other way around.

—What is the difference between the capitalist and the socialist trade?
—Capitalist trade means everything is to be sold. Socialist trade means everything is to be bought.

—What is the difference between Russian and English fairy tales?

—The English fairy tales start with 'Once upon a time . . .' and Russian fairy tales—with 'It will be soon . . .'

—We are told that the communism is already seen at the horizon." Then, what is a horizon?"
—Horizon is an imaginary line which moves away each time you approach it.

—Is it possible to build socialism in Switzerland?
—It's possible, but why? Did Switzerland really do something wrong to you?

—What is the easiest way to explain the meaning of the word 'communism'?
—By means of fists.

—Why did the man who shot at a government limousine on the Red Square miss the target?
—Because citizens who happened to be next to him tried to wrest the gun from him and shouted, 'Let me shoot!

—What is an exchange of opinions?
—When you walk into your boss's office with your opinion and walk out with his.

—What is a Soviet musical duet?
—It's a musical quartet after a trip abroad.

—Why policemen always walk the streets in teams of three?
—The partners in the police team are always chosen in such a way that one of them knows how to read, the other how to write, and the third one, naturally, has to keep watch over those two intellectuals.

—What is the difference between the Constitutions of the USA and USSR? Both guarantee freedom of speech.

—Yes, but the Constitution of the USA also guarantees freedom after the speech.

—What is permitted and what is prohibited?

—In England, what is permitted, is permitted, and what is prohibited, is prohibited.

In America everything is permitted except for what is prohibited.

In Germany everything is prohibited except for what is permitted.

In France everything is permitted, even what is prohibited.

In the USSR everything is prohibited, even what is permitted.

—Is it true that Ivanov had won last Sunday hundred thousand rubles in the state lottery?

—Yes, it is true. Only it was not last Sunday but Monday. And it was not Ivanov but Petrov. And not in the state lottery but in checkers. And not hundred thousand, but one hundred rubles. And not won but lost.

Karl Marx was resurrected and came to the USSR. He was shown factories, hospitals, cities and villages, etc. Finally, he requested to be allowed to make a speech on TV. The Politburo hesitated as they were afraid he might say something they wouldn't approve. Marx promised he would say only one sentence. Under this condition, the Politburo agreed. Karl Marx uttered the following sentence: "Workers of all countries, forgive me".

A Russian, a Frenchman and an Englishman argued about Adam's nationality. The Frenchman said, "Of course Adam was French. Look how passionately he made love to Eve!"

The Englishman said, "Of course Adam was British. Look how he gave his only apple to the lady, like a real gentleman."

The Russian said, "Of course Adam only could be Russian. Who else, possessing nothing but a sole apple, and walking with a naked ass, still believed he was in a paradise?"

In the Olympics, a Soviet hammer thrower set a new record. Correspondents interviewed him:

"How did you manage to hurl that hammer so far?"

The sportsman replied:

"If it were together with a sickle, I would send it twice as far."

A competition for the best anecdote has been announced. First prize: twenty five years in prison; second prize: twenty years in prison, and two condolence prizes: fifteen years behind the bars each.

In a prison, two inmates share their experience.

"What did they arrest you for?" one of them asks. "Was it a political or common crime?"

"Of course political. I'm a plumber. They summoned me to the district Party committee to fix the sewage pipes. I looked and said, 'Hey, the entire system requires replacement.' So, I was sentenced to seven years."

Proverbs; Proverbial Phrases; Sayings

An avaricious pays twice, a stupid pays three times, and an idiot pays all the time.

An uninvited visitor is better than an invited mother-in-law.

An uninvited guest is worse than a Tatar.

A purpose justifies the contraceptive means.

Brevity—a sister of talent, mildness—its wife, and self-interest—its mother-in-law.

Cheese is free only when it is from the trap.

Don't be rude and you will not be insulted.

Don't be so modest—you are not so great yet.

Don't regret the past—it, in fact, has not regretted you!

Don't touch other's illusions! To support of them is deceit, and to destroy them is sadism.

Happy people do not observe hours.

If you want everything and at once, you will receive nothing and gradually.

It's impossible to return to childhood—it's possible to enter one's childhood.

Jokes come and go but moods stay.

Love is a celebration of imagination above intelligence.

Love is eternal . . . only partners vary.

Life is not measured by the number of breaths we take but by the moments that take our breath away.

Money isn't a mischief—a mischief doesn't disappear so quickly.

People need money just to not think of it.

People's tastes are different:
Some love a priest, some—a priest's wife, and some—a priest's daughter.

A pessimist sees only the infinite tunnel.
An optimist sees light at the end of the tunnel.
A realist sees the tunnel, light, and a train going towards him . . .

A pessimist says that it cannot be worse, and optimist joyfully says: "It can, it can!"

Public opinion is the opinion of those who were not asked . . .

"Save money—buy a car!"
[It is a Russian proverbial phrase. Usually it took ten (10) years or more to save money and get a car for the ordinary people in the former Soviet Union]

The source of our wisdom is our experience.
The source of our experience is our foolishness.

The less letters, the more capacious the word.

The naked truth is in wine and the bitter truth is in vodka.

There is no bad without the good.

Those who got a burn from hot milk . . . blow on the cow.

Those who found a way out will trample the first . . .

Two controversial proverbs:

    1. "From two people who argue—one is a liar and another is a boor".
    2. "Truth is born from an argument".

Two proverbs that are opposite each other as well.
(first of them is probably mostly related to humans):

1. "You live and you learn".
2. "An old dog cannot be taught new tricks".

"What is good for a Russian may be deadly for a foreigner."

—An old Russian saying

Your wife will forgive and forget, but she'll never forget what she forgave.

QUESTIONS

Ballerinas are always on their toes. Why don't they just get taller ballerinas?

Can you cry under water?

Did you ever notice that when you blow in a dog's face, he gets mad at you, but when you take him for a car ride, he sticks his head out the window?

Doesn't "expecting the unexpected" make the unexpected expected?

Do Lipton employees take coffee breaks?

Friendship is one thing but what to do with libido?

Guess the riddle:
He directs the lens at you, clicks once, and you will be remembered.
Who is this?
Optimistic answer—photographer.
Pessimistic answer—sniper.

Hello, son, it's your father again. I have another question about my new computer.

Can I tape a movie from cable-TV, then fax it from my VCR to my CD-ROM, then e-mail it to my brother's cellular phone so he can make a copy on his neighbor's camcorder?

How come the dove gets to be a peace symbol? How about the pillow? It has more feathers than the dove, and it doesn't have that dangerous beak.

How come we choose from just two people to run for President and over fifty for Miss America?

How do those dead bugs get into those enclosed light fixtures?

How important does a person have to be before he is considered assassinated instead of just murdered?

How is it that we put a man on the moon before we figured out that it would be a good idea to put wheels on luggage?

Christmas . . . At what other time of the year do you sit in front of a dead tree and eat candy out of your socks?

If a deaf person has to go to court, is it still called a hearing?

If a word is misspelled in the dictionary, how would we ever know?

If corn oil is made from corn, and vegetable oil is made from vegetables, what is baby oil made from?

If love is blind, why is lingerie so popular?

If money is evil, then why aren't all poor are righteous?

If people evolved from apes, why are there still apes?

If the entire world is a stage, where is the audience sitting?

If the professor on Gilligan's Island can make a radio out of a coconut, why can't he fix a hole in a boat?

If toast always lands butter-side down, and cats always land on their feet, what happens if you fasten toast on a cat's back and drop it?

If Webster wrote the first dictionary, where did he find the words?

If we knew what it was we were doing, it would not be called research, would it?

If work is so terrific, why do they have to pay you to do it?

In what hand shouldd a gentleman hold a fork if he holds a cutlet in his right hand?

In winter time why do we try to keep the house as warm as it was in summer when we complained about the heat?

Is it good if a vacuum really sucks?

It is disgusting to see bacteria on the rim of the toilet bowl every day! But imagine what they see each day?!

I used a wrench #20 twenty times already . . . Can I use that wrench the twenty first time?

I wonder whom and how much money is necessary to give to really fight corruption.

Nowadays it is possible to change your sex, but how about a change of nationality?

So, what is the difference between networking and not working?

Statistics on sanity confirms that one out of every four people is suffering from some sort of mental illness. Think of your three best friends—if they're OK, then what about you . . .

What else to eat to lose weight?

Well, that's old age! And where is wisdom?

Where did black people come from if Adam and Eve were white, and the evolution does not exist?

Where to find a liquid from a stress relief after a removal of make-up?

Who says 'The grass is always greener on the other side'? Have you ever flipped grass over?

Why mankind came from monkeys if Eve didn't cheat Adam?

Why wise man' and 'wise guy' are opposite?

Why are they called "stands" when they are made for sitting?

Why are you IN a movie, but you're ON TV?

Why do banks charge a fee for 'insufficient funds' when they know there isn't enough money?

Why do doctors leave the room while you undress? They're going to see you naked anyway.

Why does a round pizza come in a square box?

What do I need to wish you to not be an envious later?

Why doesn't glue stick to the inside of the bottle?

Why does 'slow down' and 'slow up' mean the same thing?

Why does someone believe you when you say there're four billion stars, but doesn't check when you say the paint is wet?

Why do Kamikaze pilots wear helmets?

Why do 'overlook' and 'oversee' mean opposite things?

Why do people constantly return to the refrigerator with the hope that something new to eat will have materialized?

Why do people pay to go up tall buildings and then put money in binoculars in order to look at things on the ground?

Why do they call it an asteroid when it's outside the hemisphere, but call it a hemorrhoid when it's in your butt?

Why do they call it a TV set when you only have one?

Why do toasters always have a setting that burns the toast to a horrible crisp, which no decent human being would eat?

Why do we drive on a parkway and park on a driveway?

Why do we put suits in garment bags and garments in a suitcase?

Why do we sing 'Take me out to the ball game' when we are already there?

Why do we wash bath towels? Aren't we clean when we use them?

Why do you press harder on the buttons of a remote control when you know the batteries are going dead?

Why is 'bra' singular and 'panties' plural?

Why is it called "after dark" when it really is "after light"?

Why is it that no matter what color bubble bath you use the bubbles are always white?

Why is it that no plastic bag will open from the end on your first try?

Why is it that people say they 'slept like a baby' when babies wake up like every two hours?

Why is it that whenever you attempt to catch something that's falling off the table you always manage to knock something else over?

Why is 'phonics' is not spelled the way it sounds?

Why the third hand on the watch is called the second hand?

Why, when you talk to God it is called prayer, but when God is talking with you—schizophrenia?

Wouldn't it be nice if whenever we messed up our life we could simply press 'Ctrl Alt Delete' and start all over again?

Can you call a man a fool, who in the questionnaire, in the column labeled "DO NOT FILL", wrote "OK"?

Questions—Answers

—**C**an you describe a Russian man with German punctuality?
—A person who is always late for work by exactly two hours.

—How can you tell the difference between a dog and a wolf?

—They're spelled differently.

—Three frogs sitting on a lily, one of them decides to jump. How many frogs are left sitting on the lily?

—Three!

—That's right! Decision and action are two different things!

—What cannot be fixed?

—Something that is not broken.

—What is common between our life and a hen-house?

—Everyone aspires to sit higher up, peck at a neighbour and shit on a lower one.

—What is the difference between a boy and a man?

—The only difference is the cost of their toys.

—What is the difference between a military engineer and a civil engineer?

—A military engineer designs the weapons and a civil engineer—the targets.

—What is the difference between a toilet bowl and unison?

—It is easier to get into a toilet bowl!

—What is the difference between a TV-set and a toilet bowl?

—There is almost no difference. They show the same things. The only difference: there is better picture quality in the toilet bowl.

—What is the difference between starvation and gluttony?

—During starvation the harm is the same but there is no pleasure.

—What is the loudest string musical instrument?

—A woman's buttocks. Don't believe me? Pinch them!

—What is a freedom?

—This is what we do when no one is watching us.

—What is puberty?

—This is when it is hot and you don't know what you want more: ice cream or beer.

—What is a middle age?

—This is when you carry in bathroom not only a toilet paper but also your glasses.

When we break the law we're fined. When we act correctly we're paying taxes.

Where is the logic?

—Why are the stories with Carlson unpopular in Hollywood?

—Because he is an adult with a propeller in his butt, and in addition he is a lover of kids.

—Why does a rooster have no hands?

—Because a chicken has no tits.

—**W**hy do sculptors like to model men and women naked?

—Clothes get out of fashion, and the body always remains in demand.

—**W**hat is the difference between group sex and group therapy?

—At group therapy you hear about others problems and at group sex you see them.

—**W**here does a stork go after it brings the baby?

—It goes back to the pants.

—**W**hy did the chicken cross the road?

—To get to the other side.

—**H**ow does a computer work in a monastery begin?

—In the Name of the Father, Son and Holy Spirit—Enter!

STATEMENTS

In a country as big as Russia, New Year celebrations start somewhere in the Far East and finish somewhere under the table.

A second marriage is a triumph of hope over experience.

I have two drawbacks: laziness and a good sense of humor!
One of them constantly prevents me from living, and the other one does not allow me to die!

I don't like vodka—but I love what it does to me!

I told vodka "NO" but it doesn't want to listen . . .

Most of the things in our house are lost because my wife hides them so they don't set lost . . .

It is hard to be a man all the time . . . people interfere.

Rotor of rotor is a gradient of divergence minus Laplacian . . . Damn, why I remember this shit for fifteen years after graduation from University, but cannot remember where I put the keys yesterday!?

When it comes to the sins of others, we are judges . . . When we talk about our sins, we are lawyers!

I do not care about money! It just calms me.

I would like to personally ensure that money cannot buy happiness.

Life is beautiful if you don't remember the past and don't think about the future.

By doing nothing at work you are developing hearing, alertness and peripheral vision.

One hundred meters away to buy bread is too far.
One kilometer away to buy beer is nearby!

If there is something wrong with me, it is not your business.

If you got a spit in the back . . . then you're a step ahead!

If a Russian man decides to do nothing, nothing will stop him . . .

Happiness is when the past is not sad, the present is not annoying, and thinking about the future does not make you mad . . .

At first, we learn to talk, and then how to sit down and shut up.

Nostalgia is the desire to return something that we never had.

Romantics are the people for whom love happens more frequently than sex.

It is good not just where we aren't present but also where we have never been!

Professionals are the same as amateurs but they know where they made mistakes . . .

To mitigate the effects of the fall people commonly use obscene language.

The most important things in our lives take place in our absence.

Man needs two years in order to learn to speak and fifty years in order to learn how to be silent.

Friends come and go. Enemies accumulate.

Depression is when the air lock collapsed and crushed a builder.

Life is like a telegram, short and with errors!

People love to save money and they are willing to pay any price for it.

Stress is when you wake up screaming and all of a sudden you realize that you are not asleep.

Time is a good doctor but a poor beautician.

Old age is when the future becomes the present.

Lack of information creates a mild euphoria, and its surplus creates a severe depression.

Old age begins when more money is spent on maintaining health than on its destruction.

Someday we'll say "once upon a time . . ."

Somehow the word "truth" is involuntarily associated with the word—"terrible".

Here is a number of interesting facts to cheer you up:

1. The human heart creates pressure that can squirt blood at a distance of 10 meters. (Oh, my God!)
2. A pig's orgasm lasts 30 minutes! (I want to be a pig in my next life!)
3. A cockroach can live nine days without its head until it starves from hunger. (I still think about the pig!)
4. A male praying mantis cannot fuck having a head on its shoulders. The female initiates sex by ripping the male's head off.
5. A flea can jump 350 times the length of its body. That's like a human jumping a soccer field. (30 minutes . . . lucky pig . . . just imagine!)
6. A catfish has more than 27,000 taste buds. (And what could be so tasty on the bottom?)
7. Some lions mate over 50 times a day. (I still want to be a pig in my next life . . . quality over quantity!)
8. Butterfly taste buds are located on their feet. (Something that I always interested in . . .)
9. The strongest muscle in the body is the tongue! (Hmm . . .)
10. Right-handed people, on average, live nine years longer than left-handed people. (And if both of your hands are equally strong?)

11. Elephants are the only animals that cannot jump. (It's better than otherwise!)
12. Cat urine glows in the dark. (I wonder who paid them to find that out!?)
13. An ostrich's eye is bigger than its brain (I know some people with this problem!)
14. Sea stars have no brain (and I know such people also!)
15. Polar bears are left-handed. (They would live longer if they were retrained?)
16. Humans and dolphins are the only creatures that have sex for pleasure! (And what about the pigs?!)

*F*rom school essays:

A black guy entered the living room, red-faced from the cold.

From *Nekrasov's* books peasants learned how bad their life is . . .

Generalissimo Suvorov was a real man and slept with ordinary soldiers.

Pushkin was sensitive in many places . . .

Of all the female beauty of *Maria Bolkonsky* were her eyes.

Tractor raced across the field slightly farting . . .

We went on a camping trip in the summer for an overnight stay, and took only what was needed: potatoes, a tent and *Maria Ivanovna.*

Lensky went to a duel in his trousers. They parted, and a shot rang out.

Two horses were sons of *Taras Bulba.*

Lermontov was born in his grandmother's village house while his parents lived in St. Petersburg.

Poor Lisa picked up flowers and fed her mother.

Khlestakov sat in the cart and shouted: "Drive on, my friend, to the airport!"

Pierre was a man of the world and so peed perfumes.

Herman suddenly heard the creaking of springs. It was the old princess.

The Rostovs had three daughters: *Natasha, Sonia and Nikolay* . . .

Deaf and dumb *Gerasim* did not like gossip and told only the truth.

Gerasim ate like four strong men but worked alone.

Pugachev helped *Grinev* not only in his work but also in his love for *Masha.*

And then he took a knife and shot himself.

Boris didn't spare for a friend neither the last piece of bread nor the last bullet.

Poor Lisa picked flowers and this fed her mother.

He couldn't fall asleep all night and woke up only in the morning.

Silence—the only thing made of gold that isn't accepted by women.

You're just a treasure and I want to earth you up.

Parenting is a process of removing your personal flaws in your children.

Georgian is a title, Jewish is a vocation, Roman is a profession, and Russian is a fate.

If you have a headache, then you have a head.

No matter how many good things you do for your kids, they'll come to the cemetery no more than once a year.

Nervous is not the one who knocks his fingers on the table, and he who is annoying by that.

Sometimes an alarm clock helps to wake up but basically it disturbs sleep.

We have freedom of conscience: if you want—have conscience, and if you don't—don't have conscience.

Everybody says that we're together but only a few know where . . .

Those who know what they want, either want too little or know too much.

I hate masochists. I would beat them up again and again . . .

My imperturbability sometimes just infuriates me!

And what do these young people know about marasmus!
There is a lot in my memory, but there is nothing to tell the kids . . .

Tell me what you look like in the morning, and I'll tell you who you are.

Money is not exactly an evil—the evil doesn't disappear so quickly.

I got a monthly bill for the light at the end of the tunnel.

Whenever I remember that God is just and fair, I tremble for my country.

Freedom is not what you do or what you want, but that which you don't do
if you don't want to.

When I want to hear something clever, I start talking.

A pedestrian is always right . . . Unless he is alive.

How I love my beautiful figure, my narrow waist, my taut tummy . . .
And how I hate the layer of fat that hides it all!

I am absolutely sure that only fools can be absolutely sure of something.

There might be such a second when everything depends on a minute. And it lasts for hours.

You can somehow simulate an orgasm, but happiness—never!

I'm sorry for your interruptions while I am speaking.
Sorry for talking while you interrupt me.

—Well, if even after that disaster cockroaches remain—man said, looking at the country house that was burning down—then I do not know what to do.

In what year were you born? In what month? On what date?. And what the hell for?

You can lead a horse to water but you cannot make it drink.

Optimism is the lack of information . . .

All my life I cannot understand two things: where dust comes from and where money disappears.

Man is born to be happy, even if he is conceived by stupidity.

The Bible teaches us to love our neighbor; Kama Sutra explains how to do that.

Money is still the most popular of all printed materials.

Everything seems to be so obvious until you begin to explain it to someone.

He slept forty-two out of his seventy-two years but those years were the best of his life.

I introduced nothing new to Kama Sutra. My youth passed in vain . . .

The Earth was flat before the invention of the globe.

Some believe that genius is inherited. And others do not want to have children.

Bad is the schizophrenic who does not dream to become a paranoiac . . .

Money doesn't smell because it is laundered.

Life is given to a person once and mostly by accident.

Nothing distracts from life as much as the struggle for existence.

Life is not the days that pass but those that are remembered.

Life is 10% of what happens to us and 90% of how we react to it.

Life—this is what happens to us, as long as we make plans for the future.

Life is a sexually transmitted lethal disease.

He was smart and tried to change his life. He became wise and changed himself.

He who is afraid of nothing is risking his life. He who is afraid of everything—does not live!

Life is a good teacher, but it is too expensive to take its lessons.

The later an ambulance arrived—the more accurate is the diagnosis . . .

Nothing is more annoying than the one who you're interrupt continues talking.

The money that I earned will be enough for the rest of my life . . . if I die today at 9:00p.m.

Childhood is an age which can be shown with your fingers!

We are punished only by the gods that we pray to . . .

Husband is fed by a good wife; husband is fed up with a bad wife . . .

Some people use their last money to buy stuff that they do not need to please the people they hate.

The more he looked into the mirror, the more he believed in Darwin.

Fighting for peace is like sex for virginity.

A boy from a poor family never found out that he was allergic to caviar.

Alcohol doesn't solve any problem, but neither does milk.

I'm sorry, I hurt your feelings when I called you stupid. I really thought you already knew.

If sex between 3 people is threesome and between two people is twosome. Now I understand why people call you handsome.

I like sleeping because it's like being dead, without the commitment.

Money can't buy happiness . . . But poverty can't buy anything.

Those who say "there is no such thing as a stupid question" . . . have never worked in Customer Service.

Sometimes you have to burn a few bridges to keep the crazies from following you.

I hate when people are at your house and ask: "Do you have a bathroom?" No, we shit in the yard.

I've got to stop saying: "How stupid can you be? "Too many people are taking it as a challenge.

Not to get technical . . . But according to chemistry alcohol is a solution.

To me "drink responsibly" means don't spill it.

I'm not saying let's go kill all the stupid people . . . I'm just saying let's remove all the labels and let the problem sort itself out.

He loved her more than all the others, but he needed others to verify this.

Pinocchio: "So I had an Immaculate Conception, and my father is a carpenter . . ."

The state is a collection of individual officials, making the status of their interests the public's interests.

I have the uncomfortable feeling that you are right.

I don't know how it should be done, but you're doing it wrong.

Only those who drink know what it's like to be sober.

Objective reality is nonsense caused by lack of alcohol in blood.

STORIES

A 54 years old woman had a heart attack and was taken to the hospital. Whilst on the operating table she had a near death experience.

Seeing God she asked "Is my time up?"

God said, "No, you have another 43 years, 2 months and 8 days to live."

Upon recovery, the woman decided to stay in the hospital and have a face-lift, liposuction, breast implants and a tummy tuck. She even had someone come in and change her hair color and brighten her teeth!

Since she had so much more time to live, she figured she might as well make the most of it. After her final operation, she was released from the hospital.

Whilst crossing the street on her way home, she was killed by an ambulance.

Arriving in front of God, she demanded, "I thought you said I had another 43 years to live.

Why didn't you pull me away from the path of the ambulance?"

God replied: "I didn't recognize you!"

A crowd of people gathered around a boy who swallowed a dime.

Nobody knew what to do. A man came out of the crowd, took the boy by the legs and began to shake him. The coin dropped out.

—Are you a doctor?

—No,—answered the man,—I'm a tax inspector!

——

A drug smuggler is caught at customs with three tons of hashish.

The Russian customs officers did not catch such keif for a long time.

A group of 40 year old buddies discuss and discuss where they should meet for dinner. Finally it is agreed that they should meet at the Gausthof Zum Lowen restaurant because the waitresses there have low cut blouses and nice breasts.

10 years later, at 50 years of age, the group meets again and once again they discuss and discuss where they should meet for dinner. Finally it is agreed that they should meet at the Gausthof Zum Lowen because the food there is very good and the wine selection is good also.

10 years later at 60 years of age, the group meets again and once again they discuss and discuss where they should meet. Finally it is agreed that they should meet at the Gausthof Zum Lowen because they can eat there in peace and quiet, and the restaurant is smoke free.

10 years later, at 70 years of age, the group meets again and once again they discuss and discuss where they should meet. Finally it is agreed that they should meet at the Gausthof Zum Lowen because the restaurant is wheelchair accessible and they even have an elevator.

10 years later, at 80 years of age, the group meets again and once again they discuss and discuss where they should meet. Finally it is agreed that they should meet at the Gausthof Zum Lowen because that would be a great idea because they have never been there before.

A little American Indian boy asked his father, the big chief of the tribe, "Father, why is it that we always have long names, while the white men have shorter names like Bill, Tex or Sam?"

His father replied, "Son, our names represent a symbol, a sign, or a poem for our culture not like the white men, who live all together and repeat their names from generation to generation. Also, it is part of our makeup that in spite of everything, we survive.

For example, your sister's name is Small Romantic Moon Over The Lake, because on the night she was born, there was a beautiful moon reflected in the lake.

Then there's your brother, Big White Horse of the Prairies, because he was born on a day that the big white horse who gallops over the prairies of the world appeared near our camp and is a symbol of our capacity to live and the life force of our people. It's very simple and easy to understand.

Do you have any other questions, Little Broken Condom Made in China?

All the organs of the body were having a meeting, trying to decide who the one in charge was.

"I should be in charge," said the brain, "Because I run all the body's systems, so without me nothing would happen."

"I should be in charge," said the blood, "Because I circulate oxygen all over so without me you'd all waste away."

"I should be in charge," said the stomach," Because I process food and give all of you energy."

"I should be in charge," said the legs, "because I carry the body wherever it needs to go."

"I should be in charge," said the eyes, "Because I allow the body to see where it goes."

"I should be in charge," said the rectum, "Because I'm responsible for waste removal."

All the other body parts laughed at the rectum and insulted him, so in a huff, he shut down tight. Within a few days, the brain had a terrible headache, the stomach was bloated, the legs got wobbly, the eyes got watery, and the blood was toxic. They all decided that the rectum should be the boss.

The moral of the story? Even though the others do all the work . . . the asshole is usually in charge.

All women should live so long as to be this kind of old lady!

Toward the end of Sunday service, the Minister asked, "How many of you have forgiven your enemies?" 80% held up their hands. The Minister then repeated his question. All responded this time, except one small elderly lady . . .

"Mrs. Neely? Are you not willing to forgive your enemies?"

I don't have any . . . she replied, smiling sweetly.

"Mrs. Neely, that is very unusual. How old are you?"

"Ninety-eight", she replied. The congregation stood up and clapped their hands.

"Oh, Mrs. Neely, would you please come down in front and tell us all the secrets how a person can live ninety-eight years and not have an enemy in the world?"

The little sweetheart of a lady tottered down the aisle, faced the congregation, and said,

"I outlived the bitches."

A mailman does not dare enter the yard seeing a huge dog.

A hostess shouts:

—Don't be afraid, he is castrated!

—Yes, but I'm actually afraid that he might bite.

An American and *Rabinovich* are sitting in a compartment of a train.

The American spits on the opposite seat, the spittle turns right in the middle of it path and flies out the open window of the compartment.

—Let me introduce myself, I'm the world champion of fancy spittles.

Rabinovich spits on the opposite seat and his spittle hits a gentleman's face.

—Let me introduce myself, I'm an amateur *Rabinovich*.

An American sociologist N. has carried out research on a theme "The Attitude of People of Different Nationalities towards Another's Property". The scientist came to different cities of the world, left a suitcase in the middle of the hall of a city railway station, hid and noted the time.

In Stockholm—a suitcase was touched by nobody.

In London—a suitcase was stolen in a half an hour.

In Paris—in twenty minutes.

In Rome—in ten minutes.

In Tokyo—in five minutes a suitcase was handed over to a lost and found.

In Tel Aviv—police arrived in three minutes, surrounded the station, loaded the suitcase in an armoured vehicle and took it away from the city to blow up.

In Moscow—the operation was not a success because while the researcher looked at the suitcase his watch was stolen.

The last in the series was an experiment in Baghdad—along with the suitcase an American was stolen.

The narrator assured that the story below as a true story . . .

Scientists at NASA built a gun specifically to launch standard four (4) pound dead chickens at the windshields of airliners, military jets and the space shuttle, all travelling at maximum velocity. The idea is to simulate the frequent incidents of collisions with airborne fowl to test the strength of the windshields.

British engineers heard about the gun and were eager to test it on the windshields of their new high speed trains. Arrangements were made, and a gun was sent to the British engineers. When the gun was fired, the engineers stood shocked as the chicken hurled out of the barrel, crashed into the shatterproof shield, smashed it to smithereens, blasted through the control console, snapped the engineer's back-rest in two, and embedded itself in the back wall of the cabin, like an arrow shot from a bow.

The horrified Brits sent NASA the disastrous results of the experiment, along with the designs of the windshield and begged the US scientists for suggestions.

You're going to love this . . .

NASA responded with a one-line memo: *"Defrost the chicken."*

An intelligence officer sits on the bench with a secret service agent. The agent speaks:

—Listen! I have transferred the classified information to you! Does it mean that I'm a spy?

The intelligence officer soothes him:

—No, I'm a spy and you are simply a traitor.

An old man was sitting on a park bench enjoying the late spring sunshine when another old man sat down at the other end of the bench. They viewed each other cautiously and finally one of them heaved a tremendous, heartfelt sigh. The other rose at once and said, "If you're going to talk politics, I'm leaving."

An old mosquito was trying to bite a rubber artificial woman during the whole night.

A poet of very limited ability once complained to Oscar Wilde that critics were ignoring his latest volume:

"I'm being made the victim of a conspiracy of silence, Oscar," he said. "What should I do?"

"Join it!" said Wilde.

A wind vane has been nailed tightly—and a doomed wind blew in the specified direction.

"Dear Andy, how have you been? Your mother and I are fine. We miss you. Please sign off your computer and come downstairs for something to eat. Love, Dad."

An Englishman has a wife and a mistress—he loves the wife.
A Frenchman has a wife and a mistress—he loves the mistress.
A Jewish man has a wife and a mistress—he loves Mom.
A Russian man has a wife and a mistress—he likes to drink.
A Ukrainian man has a wife and a mistress—he simply likes to have them.

Excuse me, this money is wet because my wife strongly cried when I took it away.

Father is pointing to a big pig and says to his son:
"My son, be surprised, but don't imitate!"

"Hello, Bob? It's your father again. I have another question about my new computer.
Can I tape a movie from cable TV then fax it from my VCR to my CD-ROM then e-mail it to my brother's cell phone so he can make a copy on his neighbor's camcorder?"

—If I go along the street will there be a railway station there?
—You know, it will be there even if you don't go there.

I have said that I'm pregnant to both of them. And both have offered money for an abortion.

At this, I've regretted that I have only two of them . . .

In a personnel department:

—Do you have recommendations from a former place of work?

—Yes, I've been recommended to look for another job.

It's so good with her in bed—I fall asleep at once.

A girl had read through 'Hamlet' for the first time and was asked her opinion of it.

"Really, she said, "I don't know why people rave about it. It's nothing but a bunch of quotations strung together.

—How has their divorce case ended?

—It has ended as usual. Husband got the car, his spouse got the children, and the lawyer got all the rest as the fee.

I have a misfortune—my Persian cat has made a Persian Gulf on my Persian rug.

It was spring, the weather was delightful, and a man on a park bench breathed deeply and listened to the melodious chirping of numerous birds. Turning to the stranger who happened to be sharing the bench with him, he said, "Isn't the music of the birds delightful?"

The other man scowled and said, "How the devil can I hear what you're saying over the damned noise of those stupid birds?"

I've lent a familiar person five thousand dollars for his plastic surgery, and now I don't know what he looks like!

Jerusalem. An American tourist arrives and wishes to get to the Western Wall but he does not know what it is called. He stops a taxi and says to the taxi driver:
"Bring me to the place where you, Jews, cry, shout and knock your heads against a wall . . ."
The driver brought him to a Tax Police building.

Kalashnikov said at his jubilee that he was always surrounded by kind and good people and because of them he created his famous weapons.

Mice cried, were pricked but continue to guzzle **a** cactus . . .

Mohammed and *Abdul* are two friends who beg alms in different areas of London. *Abdul* brings home a handful of small coins every evening whereas Mohammed comes back home with a suitcase full of £10 coins every evening. He has a house with paid mortgage, and there is a Mercedes in his garage.
Once *Abdul* asked Mohammed:
"Tell me, why does it turn out that I work not less than you, assiduously collect alms but I bring home much less than you?
"Tell me now what is written on your tablet with which you collect alms?"—Mohammed asked. "I'm unemployed and contain my wife and six children. Help me, please!"
"No wonder that you collect just a few pounds a day."—Mohammed exclaimed.
"And what is written on your tablet?"—*Abdul* asked.

"I need just £10 to come back home to Pakistan."—Mohammed answered.

Mrs. Jones consults a psychiatrist.

"My husband," she said, "is convinced he's a chicken. He goes around squawking constantly and sleeps on a large bar of wood he has fixed up as a perch."

"I see, said the psychiatrist thoughtfully. "And how long has your husband been suffering from this fixation?

"For two years now."

The psychiatrist frowned slightly and said, "But why have you waited till now to seek help?"

Mrs. Jones blushed and said, "Oh, well—it was so nice having a steady supply of eggs."

A man brought his wife to a psychologist with the complaint that there are no sexual relationships between them for about a year.

The psychologist asks him to leave his office temporarily and begins to persistently prick the woman. Eventually she confesses:

—Recently my husband was laid off. There's not enough money . . .

Every morning I go to work by taxi. The driver always asks me: "Well, are you going to pay or as usual!?" Well, I choose 'as usual'. 'As usual' takes too long and I'm late for work.

My chief gets me to talk in his office and asks: "Well, dismiss you or as usual!?"

Again I choose 'as usual'. Then I go back home by taxi and again I choose 'as usual'. Eventually, I simply get tired and just physically cannot satisfy my husband. Doctor, help me!

Doctor:

—Well, either I'll tell all this to your husband or as usual . . .

A man comes into a sex-shop and, hesitating, is interested:

—Have you got a rubber woman?

—Yes, certainly!

—Does it get warm?

—Yes, there is a temperature regulator.

—And, can it scratch?

—Here is a breaker lever, you can pull it . . .

—And I still want it to shout.

—Please, here is a loudness regulator!

—Well, I'll take it, could you, please, wrap it up for me?

Next day he brings it back.

—What happened, was it not warm?

—It was hot (shows burns on his chest).

—Did it scratch?

—Yes, everything is OK with it (shows a scratched back and a neck).

—So, doesn't it shout?

—It shouted so the neighbors knocked on the wall!

—And, why do you hand it back?

—She hasn't given!

('give' means female permission to have sex with her in Russian slang)

A client is sitting in the chair in a barber shop and all of a sudden notices that the barber's dog looks at him very attentively. He asks the barber:

—Why is your dog looking at me this way?

—Because sometimes client ears drop down on the floor along with the hairs . . .

My cat urinates in corners very frequently and I beat him but it seems to me that he thinks that I beat him because he urinates not enough.

Nervous I became recently. Nervous . . .
My wife tells me that it's because I drink muck.
Actually it's time to change.
Today I'll try a calming lotion after shaving . . .

Night in America. Silence. The only thing audible is the prices falling on real estate.

During a fashion show one man sneezed and blew three models off of a podium.

Once, I looked and there was a large bolt screwed in front below my belt.
I unscrewed it and . . . my buttocks fell off . . .

One morning, the husband returns the boat to their lakeside cottage after several hours of fishing and decides to take a nap.
Although not familiar with the lake, the wife decides to take the boat out.
She motors out a short distance, anchors, puts her feet up, and begins to read her book.
The peace and solitude are magnificent. Along comes a Fish and Game Warden in his boat.
He pulls up alongside the woman and says,
'Good morning, Ma'am. What are you doing?
'Reading a book,' she replies, (thinking, 'Isn't that obvious?')
'You're in a Restricted Fishing Area,' he informs her.
'I'm sorry, officer, but I'm not fishing. I'm reading.'
'Yes, but I see you have all the equipment.
For all I know you could start at any moment.

I'll have to take you in and write you up.'

If you do that, I'll have to charge you with sexual assault,' says the woman.

'But I haven't even touched you,' says the Game Warden.

'That's true, but you have all the equipment. For all I know you could start at any moment.'

'Have a nice day ma'am,' and he left.

MORAL:

Never argue with a woman who reads.

It's likely she can also think.

Phone call to the tech support:

—I cannot open the Internet . . .

—Is the light on the modem on?

—Yes. But it isn't the light, it's a thyristor LED.

—Well, there is, probably, a problem on our side.

A man is walking down the street, and suddenly sees an accident: people are covered in blood, the cars are broken. *The man* approaches one of the wounded men and asks:

—Has the insurance agent already come?

—Not yet.

—Well, then I'll lie down near you.

She looked in the mirror and put one more bottle of vodka on the table.

She spent the first day packing her belongings into boxes, crates and suitcases.

On the second day, she had the movers come and collect her things.

On the third day, she sat down for the last time at their beautiful dining room table by candle-light, put on some soft background music, and feasted on a pound of shrimp, a jar of caviar, and a bottle of spring-water.

When she had finished, she went into each and every room and deposited a few half-eaten shrimp shells dipped in caviar into the hollow of the curtain rods.

She then cleaned up the kitchen and left . . . When the husband returned with his new girlfriend, all was bliss for the first few days.

Then slowly, the house began to smell.

They tried everything; cleaning, mopping and airing the place out.

Vents were checked for dead rodents and carpets were steam cleaned.

Air fresheners were hung everywhere. Exterminators were brought in to set off gas canisters, during which they had to move out for a few days and in the end they even paid to replace the expensive wool carpeting.

Nothing worked!

People stopped coming over to visit.

Repairmen refused to work in the house.

The maid quit.

Finally, they could not take the stench any longer and decided to move.

A month later, even though they had cut their price in half, they could not find a buyer for their stinky house.

Word got out and eventually even the local realtors refused to return their calls.

Finally, they had to borrow a huge sum of money from the bank to purchase a new place.

The ex-wife called the man and asked how things were going.

He told her the saga of the rotting house. She listened politely and said that she missed her old home terribly and would be willing to reduce her divorce settlement in exchange for getting the house.

—

277

Knowing his ex-wife had no idea how bad the smell was, he agreed on a price that was about 1/10th of what the house had been worth, but only if she were to sign the papers that very day.

She agreed and within the hour his lawyers delivered the paperwork.

A week later the man and his girlfriend stood smiling as they watched the moving company pack everything to take to their new home . . .

And to spite the ex-wife, they even took the curtain rods!

Tell the parachutists to stop jumping. We haven't taken off yet.

The bride was so funny . . . She played *balalaika* and ate seeds at the same time.

Our plane crew says goodbye to all of you and wishes you a pleasant flight.

There is a scandal at the zoo: the director documented a dead elephant as a sleeping one and received money for its feeding.

Tomorrow the Russian televiewers will not be able to see the weather forecast . . .

Coffee grounds have not been delivered.

Two sardines were startled, in the depth of the ocean, when a submarine glided by. Said one, "Heavens, what's that?" "Nothing," said the other. "Just a can of people."

We were fighting alcoholism yesterday!

I don't remember the details but there's a feeling that drunkenness won with a great advantage.

What a nasty thing! Wrap up five pieces for me, please.

—**W**hat does a cock think when he chases a hen?
—If I don't catch her I'll warm myself up!

Yesterday my grandmother sat in chair knitting when a bared electric power cord dropped . . . My grandmother continued to knit but with a frequency of 50 Hz.

A woman opened the front door and saw a workman standing on the porch, carrying a box of tools.
"I'm a piano tuner ma'am"—he announced.
"But I didn't order a piano tuner's service."
"I know, but the neighbors did!"
Yesterday on the TV program "Good night, kids" a puppeteer accidentally hit his head on the table. The children never heard such wishes for the night.

Intellectual family. 17-year-old daughter is pregnant. All are in shock, her mother drinks sedative medication and wipes away a tear, father grimly drinks Martel. Everyone is waiting for the arrival of the culprit. Red Ferrari stops at the entrance, a staid man gets out of the car. He enters the apartment, stopping all parents' oohs and aahs and says:
—Well, I'm a very famous person, I have a family and I cannot leave them. However, I won't leave your daughter as well. I decided so. If your daughter will give birth to a boy he will inherit my two factories which cost $20 million dollars and a Harvard education, and your daughter will have a permanent alimony of $2 million dollars a year. If she gives birth to a girl she will inherit my factory, $10 million dollars and an Oxford education. Your daughter will have a permanent alimony of $1 million a year.

———

And in case of miscarriage!. Here her father stands up, puts his glass on the table, approaches the man, puts his hand on his shoulder and says:

-Then you fuck her again!

Morning in a respectable English family:

Sir is sitting in a chair with a newspaper over morning coffee. Lady goes down the stairs from her bedroom and says:

—Bad news, sir. What we thought was a pregnancy is not a pregnancy.

—So, lady, we will not have an heir?

—Sorry, sir . . .

—Oh my God! Again, with these absurd body movements!

A student of the music school for the first time in his role as an entertainer, in great agitation announces: "Now a freshman *Natasha Orlova* will perform Chopin's 'Desire'."

Today I wanted to jump out the window but then I thought that decent women do not lay on the street and decided to limit my hysteria!

I received a photo from the traffic police where I was exceeding the speed limit.

I sent them a video where I pay a fine to the traffic cop in cash.

When I was little, I asked God for a bike. Then I realized that God works differently . . . and then I stole a bike and begged God for forgiveness.

A man approaches a hotel hostess and says:

—There's no cold water in my room.

—Well, wait.

—What should I wait for?

—While the hot water gets cool.

It seems everything is OK: I got a job, bought a car and an apartment, got money for a mistress, and all of a sudden . . . I'm already 70 years old!

Written message received by a performer from a person sitting in the audience:

"Thank you very much! I do not regret the time that I lost in vain!"

My husband came home tired, so spousal duty was paid in cash.

Mother's parting words before the wedding:

"Daughter, never argue with your husband! Immediately cry!"

Once, a kind man talked to God and asked him:

—God, I'd like to know what Heaven is and what Hell is.

Lord led him to two doors, opened one of them and invited him inside.

There was a huge round table in the middle of which a huge bowl filled with various meals that smelled delicious had been placed.

People sitting around the table looked hungry and sick. They all looked hungry. All of them were holding spoons with long handles attached to their hands. They could get a cup filled with food and grab it but because the spoon's handles were too long no one could bring a spoon to the mouth.

The kind man was shocked to see their trouble.

Lord said:

—You've just seen Hell.

Lord and the kind man went to the second door then. Lord opened it. The kind man saw the scene that was identical to the previous one. There was a huge round table, the same giant bowl that made his mouth fill with saliva. People sitting around the table were holding the same spoons with very long handles. Only this time they looked well fed, happy and absorbed in pleasant conversations with each other.

The kind man said to the Lord:

—I don't understand.

—It's pretty simple,—said Lord to him. These people have learned to feed each other. The others think only of themselves.

Heaven and Hell have the same structure. The difference is in us.

Before pregnancy, I was sleeping on my stomach!

During pregnancy—on the side!

After giving birth I can sleep just by standing!

Organizers of the exhibition of Picasso assured viewers that they can enjoy the works of the artist even if they are sober.

Yesterday, my wife managed to burn 5,000 calories in one hour. Along with them she burned a cooking pan in which she cooked food.

In general, the situation is classic:

A wife is in bed with a weary lover. All of a sudden the husband enters the room.

The wife turns to the lover and is screaming:

—Dear! Prove him that you're a real man!

The lover (perplexedly):

—How? And to him, also?

A single beggar man living in a shared apartment with his blind mother in their daily prayers asks God to improve his life . . . Finally, God decides to grant his prayers, performing only one single wish.

The man says:

—Thank you, Lord! My only wish is that my Mom would see how my wife is hanging the twenty millionth necklace around the neck of my daughter in my six hundredth Mercedes that is parked next to a pool in my Beverly Hills mansion!

An incident in paradise:

—Lord, here are the atheists for you!

—Tell them that I do not exist.

A queen had a headache all the time, because her head was growing and her crown wasn't.

In his 20 years, he knew six operating systems and no women.

I bought an audio course "English in a dream". The whole year before bedtime I listened to the cassette.

The result is somewhat unexpected: at the sound of the English language I instantly fall asleep.

A farmer drove to a neighbor's farmhouse and knocked at the door.

A boy, about 9, opened the door.

"Is your dad or mom home?" asked the farmer.

"No, they went to town" said the boy.

"How about your brother, Howard? Is he here?" asked the farmer.

"No, he went with Mom and Dad" the boy answered.

The farmer stood there for a few minutes, shifting from one foot to the other, and mumbling to himself.

"I know where all the tools are, if you want to borrow one, or I can give Dad a message"—said the boy.

"Well," said the farmer uncomfortably, "I really wanted to talk to your Dad. It's about your brother Howard getting my daughter Suzy pregnant".

The boy thought for a moment . . .

"You would have to talk to Dad about that. I know he charges $500 for the bull and $50 for the pig, but I don't know how much he charges for Howard."

Three unknown men robbed a passerby and took his passport. The passport was torn. So there became four unknown men . . .

A little girl is crying in the pharmacy:

—My mother sent me for the medicine, and I forgot its name. It is short and simple . . . I only remember that it is composed of hydroxymethyllaminotrifenilatsetat.

Two friends meet each other. One of them is on crutches.

—What happened to you?

—I was in a car accident.

—What a mess! So now you cannot walk without crutches, can you?

—Who knows! The doctor said that I can, and the attorney said that I cannot.

After landing my new job as a Wal-Mart greeter, a good find for many retirees, I lasted less than a day . . .

About two hours into my first day on the job a very loud, decidedly unattractive, woman walked into the store along with her two kids, yelling obscenities at them all the way through the entrance.

As I had been instructed, I said, pleasantly, "Good morning and welcome to Wal-Mart."

I then said, "Nice children you have there. Are they twins?"

The ugly woman stopped yelling long enough to say "Don't be fucking stupid. Of course they aren't twins. The oldest one's 9, and the other one's 7."

"Why the hell would you think they're twins? Are you blind, or just stupid?"

I replied, "I'm neither blind nor stupid, Madam. I just couldn't believe someone fucked you twice.

Have a good day and thank you for shopping at Wal-Mart."

My supervisor said I probably wasn't cut out for this line of work.

The manager asks:

—Do you have any experience as a seller?

The young man willingly responds:

—Of course! I worked as a salesman!

The manager clearly liked the young man:

—Start working right now.

The first day was very stressful but the young man handled it.

At the end of the working day the manager came up to him and asked:

—Well, how many people made purchases today?

—One.

—One? A salesperson at the mall provides customer service for an average of 20 to 30 purchases per day! Yeah! And how much money did your customer leave?

—$102,516 and ¢17.

—What-oh-oh? $102,516 and ¢17? What did you sell him?

—First, I sold him a small fish hook, then a medium one and then he bought the largest hook. Then I sold him the most fashionable bait. When these purchases were packed I asked where he was going fishing. He replied at Finnish Gulf. To which I told him that he needs a boat for fishing. We went down to the boat department and I advised him to buy a twin-engine boat. He liked it, but he doubted that his sports car will be able to tow the boat. We went to the automotive section, and then I advised him to buy a jeep with a trailer. These are the purchases my first client made today.

The manager, with his square eyes, followed the story told by the new salesman:

—Do you mean that the buyer came to buy a fish hook, and eventually bought a boat and a jeep with a trailer?

—No, no. He stopped by to buy a pack of tampons for his wife. And I told him that now the weekend cannot be spent properly anyway, so it's better to go fishing . . .

Two lawyers come into the coffee shop, order drinks and take out sandwiches from their bags.

—Sorry,—says the bartender—but you cannot eat your own food here.

The attorneys look at each other, shrug and . . . exchange their sandwiches.

The opinions of the members of the jury on the question "What is sex":

President: "Sex is a disease since it requires bed rest."

Doctor: "What kind of illness is it if it consumes so much energy? It is work!"

Engineer: "What kind of work is it when all lay down and an instrument of production is working? It's a process."

Lawyer: "What kind of process is it if one gives the other? It's a bribe!"

Prosecutor: "What kind of a bribe is it if the two are satisfied? This is an art!"

Actress: "What art is it if there is no audience? This is science!"

Professor: "What kind of science is it if the lousiest student can do it? This is a bargain!"

Jewish: "You'll have to excuse me but what kind of deal is it if you invest more and take out less? It's a robbery!"

I was so depressed last night thinking about the economy, wars, jobs, my savings, Social Security, retirement funds, etc., I called the Suicide Hotline. I got a call center in Pakistan, and when I told them I was suicidal, they got all excited, and asked if I could drive a truck.

SUDDENLY HE REALIZED HE WAS IN LINE FOR A JOB INSTEAD OF FOOD STAMPS ...

At the customs control of an airport a dog, trained to find drugs, made it clear several times that a passenger's problem can be easily solved with the exchange of one kilo of steak.

The starter was a former sniper, and the runners knew that ...

A man is walking along the street and suddenly his watch breaks. He spots a shop window across the street with a big clock in it. He enters the shop and sees a Jewish man with a big beard who is sitting at the desk.

—Do you fix watches?

—No, we do circumcisions ...

—And, why is there the clock in your showcase?

—And what do you suggest we hang in it?

An old woman was asked,

"At your ripe age, what would you prefer to get,

Parkinsons or Alzheimers?"

The wise lady answered,

"Definitely Parkinsons—better to spill half my wine than to forget where I keep the bottle."

She confused contraceptives and soothing pills . . .

She now has nine children, but she worries little about them.

Today at seven in the morning at a local hospital in a Moscow suburb, Mrs. *Ivanov* gave birth to five girls. The doctors hope they can save the life of Mr. *Ivanov*.

A loud cry at the temple:

—Brothers, I can walk again! I can walk again!

—Tell us, how did the miracle happen?

—They stole my car!

A defence lawyer asks the plaintiff:

—And you're absolutely sure, that my client stole your car?

—Well, after your fiery speech, I'm not sure that I had a car!

Adam came home late in the evening. Eve jealously asks:

—Where have you been?

—Honey, don't you know that we are alone in heaven?

But every night after that Eve, just in case, examined and re-counted his ribs.

A zoo keeper escaped from the zoo . . . But, perhaps, the lions didn't tell the whole story.

A prison governor addresses a suicide bomber who is sitting on the electric chair:

What is your last wish?

—Please hold my hand. I'll be much quieter.

A coach comforts a boxer who lost the fight:

—And yet your rival was scared in the third round.

—How's that?

—He thought he killed you.

Two drunk Jews knock into the gates of a convent, obviously not knowing where they are. Behind the gate women are shouting at them:

—Get out of here! We are the brides of Christ, and who are you?

—We? We are the relatives from the groom's side!

Newcomer asks the skydiving instructor:

—What if the main parachute does not open up and the reserve parachute does not open upeither, how long will I fly to the earth?

—For the rest of your life ...

As a child, the future great physiologist Pavlov's was bitten by a dog. The dog bit him and forgot about that. But Pavlov grew up and did not forget.

—**D**oes your bank give loans on parole?

—No problem ...

—What if I do not return?

—You will be ashamed before God when you appear before Him.

—Oh, it will be not very soon ...

—No, if you don't return on May the 5-th, you will appear before Him on May the 6-th.

A witness was called to appear at the session of the court by a letter. The witness's letter returned back with a note: "The addressee is dead." Wanting to check this message, the court clerk sent a secondary invitation. This time the letter came back with a note: "The addressee is still dead."

My grandfather ate only vegetables, yogurt, boiled fish and other healthy foods every day. He got up at 6:00 am and went to bed at 10 pm, did gymnastics, did not drink, did not smoke, was moderate in sex, and died at age 90 . . . of boredom.

I signed up for an exercise class and was told to wear loose fitting clothing. If I HAD any loose fitting clothing, I wouldn't have signed up in the first place!

She says that it was in ecstasy, but I seem to remember that it was in the shed . . .

The biologist *Nikolaev* derived a new breed of pigeons.
Smart birds fly to the exact address shown on the envelope, and crap there.

And Lord said to the people: "Be fruitful and multiply!"
And He repeated the phrase three times for Chinese.

A senior official who hit two pedestrians crossing the street, asks a judge about the possible sentence.
—Well,—says the judge,—I guess that the one who smashed the windshield with his head can get 5 years behind bars for the damage to property and for

the attempted theft. And the second one, who bounced into the bushes, may get 8 years in jail for attempting to escape from the scene.

He was so lazy that he even married an already pregnant girl.

The New York City branch of Bank Leumi decides to carry out an audit of passwords used by their customers. To their surprise, they find that Harry Levy, one of their elderly customers, has regularly been using a very lengthy password.

The password being used was: *AdamEveNoahMosesAbrahamIsaacJacobJosephJerusalem*
So the office manager phones Harry.

"Mr. Levy," says the manager, "we've just discovered that you're using an unnecessarily long password to get into your online account with us. Why did you choose such a long password?"

"I only did what I was instructed to do by your office," replies Harry.

"So what did they tell you to do?" asks the manager.

Harry replies, "They told me that the password had to be eight characters long and had to include at least one capital."

The day after his wife disappeared in a kayaking accident, an Anchorage man answered his door to find two grim-faced Alaska State Troopers.

"We're sorry Mr. Page, but we have some information about your wife," said one trooper . . .

"Tell me! Did you find her?" Page shouted.

The troopers looked at each other.

One said, "We have some bad news, some good news, and some really great news. Which do you want to hear first?"

Fearing the worst, an ashen Mr. Page said, "Give me the bad news first."

The trooper said, "I'm sorry to tell you, sir, but this morning we found your wife Gerry's body in Kachemak Bay."

"Oh my God!" exclaimed Page. Swallowing hard, he asked, "What's the good news?"

The trooper continued, "When we pulled her up, she had 12 twenty-five pound king crabs and 6 good-size Dungeness crabs clinging to her and we feel you are entitled to a share in the catch."

Stunned, Mr. Page demanded, "If that's the good news, what's the great news?"

The trooper said, "We're going to pull her up again tomorrow."

Two Jewish men are sitting on a park bench. A bird, flying over, discharges its drop, which hits one of them on the shoulder.

"Did you see that?" the man who was hit asks, rubbing his arm. "And for the Russians, they sing."

A programmer needs to go to the 12th floor. He enters the elevator, pushes 1, then he pushes 2, and then he begins to frantically search for the 'Enter' button.

At a busy bus stop, a woman who was waiting for a bus was wearing a tight leather skirt. As the bus stopped and it was her turn to get on, she became aware that her skirt was too tight to allow her leg to come up to to the height of the first step of the bus.

Slightly embarrassed and with a quick smile to the bus driver, she reached behind her to unzip her skirt a little, thinking that this would give her enough slack to raise her leg. Again, she tried to make the step only to discover she still couldn't.

So, a little more embarrassed, she once again reached behind her to unzip her skirt a little more.

For the second time, attempted the step, and, once again, much to her chagrin, she could not raise her leg. With little smile to the driver, she again reached behind to unzip a little more and again was unable to make the step.

About this time, a large man who was standing behind her picked her up easily by the waist and placed her gently on the step of the bus. She went ballistic and turned to the would-be Samaritan and screeched, "How dare you touch my body! I don't even know who you are!'

The man smiled and drawled, "Well, ma'am, normally I would agree with you, but after you unzipped my fly three times, I kinda figured we was friends."

—How many times does a woman blush in her life?

—Four times: on the wedding night, when she is cheating for the first time, when she takes money for the first time, and when she gives money for the first time.

—And what about a man?

—Twice: the first time—when he cannot the second, and the second time—when he cannot the first time.

A nondescript man and a woman of stunning beauty enter a jewelry store late in the evening. The man asks the owner of the store:

—Good evening. We are interested in this diamond necklace.

—Please, it costs $ 25,000

The man pulls out a checkbook and writes a check.

The owner is in some disarray.

The man is tries to explain to him:

—I understand. The banks are closed now, and you would like to receive a confirmation of receipt. Let's do this: we leave the check and the necklace here in the store, you call tomorrow morning to the bank, get a confirmation of receipt, call me and I'll come to pick up the necklace . . .

The next morning, the man the phone rings.

The shop owner:

—I'm sorry, but the bank refuses to confirm your check.

The man:

—No problem. Tear up the check, put the necklace back, and don't worry, I already slept with this woman yesterday . . .

Tasteless humor, but maybe it'll make someone laugh:

"I saw a one legged Muslim with no arms at the ATM today.

He asked me to check his balance . . . so I pushed the fucker over."

Suddenly he realized he was in line for a job instead of food stamps . . .

A Russian and an American die and they both go to hell. Satan asks them, "Which hell do you prefer, the Russian or American?"

"What's the difference?" the Russian asks.

"In the American hell, you will be forced to eat one bucket of waste every day; in the Russian, two," Satan explains.

The American decides to go to the American hell. The Russian, being a patriot, chooses the Russian hell.

One year later the two men run into one another. "How's life?" the Russian asks.

"Can't complain," the American answers. "I eat one bucket of waste every morning, and then I'm free for the rest of the day. What about you?"

"It couldn't be better!" the Russian explains. "Just like back on earth! They're either late with waste deliveries, or they're having bucket shortages."

A Soviet judge walks out of the courtroom, barely managing to suppress his wild laughter.

A colleague asks, "What is it you're laughing about?"

"Well, I just heard a great joke," the judge says.

"A joke? Tell me!"

"Are you crazy? I just sentenced a man to five years for that joke!"

After having a few drinks, two friends are talking outside a bar:

"I know an address where we can have a corking good time tonight," says one. "There are two girls. One of them is really good-looking. She's mine. The second one . . . well, after you get a few more shots of vodka into you, you'll find her acceptable."

"Okay, let's go," agrees the other.

The friends arrive at their destination. The doors open, and there they see two young women, just waiting for them. The less fortunate friend pauses to look at the women, then turns to his friend and says, rather skeptically, "It's not going to work, buddy. I can't drink that much!"

An elderly lady was invited to an old friend's home for dinner one evening. She was impressed by the way her friend preceded every request to her husband with endearing terms such as: Honey, My Love, Darling, Sweetheart, etc. The couple had been married almost 70 years and, clearly, she was still very much in love. While the husband was in the living room, the friend leaned over to her hostess and said: 'I think it's wonderful that, after all these years, you still call your husband such loving names.'

—

The elderly lady hung her head. 'I have to tell you the truth,' she said, 'his name slipped my mind about a year ago and I'm scared to death to ask the cranky old asshole what it is.'

A talented artist asked his gallery owner if anyone had shown interest in his paintings.

"I've got good news and bad news," she said. "The good news is that some guy inquired if your work will appreciate in value after you die. When I told him that it would, he bought all 15 of your original paintings. He spent 4.9 million dollars on your paintings."

"That's awesome," exclaims the artist. "I can now retire in wealth. And the bad news?"

"That guy was your doctor."

An elderly lady sits in a pothole alongside a sidewalk, murmuring the same phrase over and over again:" I've lost it! I've lost it! . . ."

A passerby stops to give her a hand. "What is it that you have lost?" he asks the lady.

"My balance," the lady answers. "I've lost my balance!"

An attorney telephoned the governor just after midnight, insisting that he talk to him regarding a matter of utmost urgency.

An aide eventually agreed to wake up the governor.

"So, what is it?" grumbled the governor.

"Judge has just died," said the attorney, "and I want to take his place."

The governor replied: "Well, it's OK with me if it's OK with the undertaker."

A mechanic was removing a cylinder-head from the motor of a Harley motorcycle when he spotted a well-known cardiologist in his shop. The cardiologist was there waiting for the service manager to come take a look at his bike when the mechanic shouted across the garage, "Hey Doctor, want to take a look at this?"

The cardiologist, a bit surprised, walked over to where the mechanic was working on the motorcycle. The mechanic straightened up, wiped his hands on a rag and said, "So Doc, look at this engine. I open its heart, take the valves out, repair any damage, and then put them back in, and when I finish, it works just like new.

So how come I make $80,000 a year, a pretty small salary, and you earn a hefty $460,000 when you and I are basically doing the same work?"

The cardiologist paused, smiled and leaned over, then whispered to the mechanic, "Try doing it with the engine running!"

Sherlock Holmes and Dr Watson were going camping. They pitched their tent under the stars and went to sleep. Sometime in the middle of the night Holmes woke Watson up and said: "Watson, look up at the stars, and tell me what you see." Watson replied: "I see millions and millions of stars." Holmes said: "And what do you deduce from that?" Watson replied: "Well, if there are millions of stars, and if even a few of those have planets, it's quite likely there are some planets like Earth out there. And if there are a few planets like Earth out there, there might also be life." And Holmes said: "Watson, you idiot, it means that somebody stole our tent."

An old Armenian is on his deathbed:

—My children, treasure the Jews.

—Why Jews?

—Because once they are dealt with, we will be next.

A traffic policeman stops a car.

The policeman asks the driver, "Have you drunk vodka today?"

Driver: "No."

Policeman: "Breathe into the tube . . . Well, no alcohol is detected . . . Maybe the tube is broken . . . (breathes into the tube himself) No, it's working!"

You stop your car to pick up a random traveler—a beautiful girl, who signals from the road. The girl suddenly faints. You take her to the hospital. This is stress.

At the hospital, they tell you that she is pregnant and congratulate you with your future paternity. You explain that you first saw her an hour ago, but they insist that you are the father. This is a lot of stress.

You are required to take a DNA test for paternity. After the test results come in, the doctor tells you that you cannot be a father because you are genetically fruitless. This news causes stress, mixed with relief.

On the way home you recall that you have three children. Here you experience THE REAL STRESS.

Greg: "Your new secretary is very sexy . . . ."

Sergey: "Thanks! She's actually a robot, named Dasha . . . .

If you squeeze her right breast, she takes dictation & if you squeeze her left breast, she types letters.

Will work as long as you like, no complaining, no sick days, no medical, no dental . . . .

I'll lend her to you for a day & you can see how functional and efficient she is".

Next day, Greg calls Sergey from the hospital & shouts:

"Sergey . . . . You bastard!

You didn't tell me that the hole between Dasha's legs is a Pencil Sharpener . . ."

An elderly couple had just learned how to send text messages on their cell phones.

The wife was a romantic type and the husband was more of a no-nonsense guy.

One afternoon the wife went out to meet a friend for coffee. She decided to send her husband a romantic text message and she wrote:

"If you are sleeping, send me your dreams.

If you are laughing, send me your smile.

If you are eating, send me a bite.

If you are drinking, send me a sip.

If you are crying, send me your tears.

I love you."

The husband texted back to her: "I'm on the toilet.

Please advise."

A hiker stopped at the bank of a fast-flowing river. Spying a simple fellow standing on the opposite bank, he yelled to him, "How do I get to the other side?"

The simpleton scratched his head. He looked up the river. He looked down the river. Then he yelled back to the hiker, "You're already ON the other side!"

Universal Laws

Brown's Law of Physical Appearance:

If the clothes fit, they are ugly.

Doctor's Law:

If you don't feel well, make an appointment to go to the doctor. By the time you get there you'll feel better. Don't make an appointment, and you'll stay sick.

Law of Biomechanics:

The severity of the itch is inversely proportional to the reach.

Law of Close Encounters:

The probability of meeting someone you know increases dramatically when you are with someone you don't want to be seen with.

Law of Gravity:

Any tool, nut, bolt, screw, when dropped, will roll to the least accessible corner.

Law of Logical Argument:

Anything is possible if you don't know what you are talking about.

Law of Mechanical Repair:

After your hands become coated with grease, your nose will begin to itch and you'll have to pee.

Law of Physical Surfaces:

The chances of an open-faced jelly sandwich landing down on a floor covering are directly correlated to the newness and cost of the carpet/rug.

Law of Probability:

The probability of being watched is directly proportional to the stupidity of your act.

Law of Random Numbers:

If you dial a wrong number, you never get a busy signal and someone always answers.

Law of the Alibi:

If you tell the boss you were late for work because you had a flat tire, the very next morning you will have a flat tire.

Law of the Bath:

When the body is fully immersed in water—the telephone rings.

Law of the Result:

When you try to prove to someone that a machine won't work, it will.

Law of the Theater and Hockey Arena:

At any event, the people whose seats are furthest from the aisle arrive last and they are the ones who will leave their seats several times to go for food, beer, or the toilet and who leave early before the end of the performance or the game is over while those in the aisle seats come early, never move once, have long gangly legs or big bellies and who stay to the bitter end of the performance and beyond. The aisle people also are very surly folk.

Murphy's Law of Lockers:
If there are only two people in a locker room, they will have adjacent lockers.

Oliver's Law of Public Speaking:
A closed mouth gathers no feet.

Starbucks Law:
As soon as you sit down to a cup of hot coffee, your boss will ask you to do something which will last until the coffee is cold.

Variation Law:
If you change lines (or traffic lanes), the one you were in will always move faster than the one you are in now (works every time).

Wilson's Law of Commercial Marketing Strategy:
As soon as you find a product that you really like, they will stop making it.

WISHES

Message sent to TV program:

"I ask you to not start up an advertising running line at the bottom of the screen during the news! My mother-in-law thinks that it is karaoke text and sings!"

Dear Royal Academy in Stockholm!

Give me any Nobel Prize, for instance, on the economy . . .

In fact, for the last half a century I have not provoked any financial crisis and did not try to stop progress.

Dear women!

Congratulations on International Women's Day on March the 8th!

Let every day be the Day of March the 8th and every night be the Day of February 23rd!

[These two very popular holidays in former Soviet Union continue to be celebrated by Russians even now. People began to celebrate the first before the WWI (mostly in the countries of Eastern Europe); the second one is a national holiday—the Soviet Army's Day]

For full happiness it would be desirable to survive . . .

New Year Wishes:

May your hair, your teeth, your face-lift, your abs and your stocks not fall; and may your blood pressure, your triglycerides, your cholesterol, your white blood count and your mortgage interest not rise.

May you get a clean bill of health from your dentist, your cardiologist, your gastroenterologist, your urologist, your proctologist, your podiatrist, your psychiatrist and your plumber.

May what you see in the mirror delight you, and what others see in you delight them.

May someone love you enough to forgive your faults, be blind to your blemishes, and tell the world about your virtues.

May New Year's Eve find you seated around the table, together with your beloved family and cherished friends.

May you find the food better, the environment quieter, the cost much cheaper, and the pleasure much more fulfilling than anything else you might ordinarily do that night.

May the telemarketers wait to make their sales calls until you finish dinner, may the commercials on TV not be louder than the program you have been watching, and may your check book and your budget balance—and include generous amounts for charity.

May you remember to say "I love you" at least once a day to your spouse, your child, your parent, and your siblings; but not to your secretary, your nurse, your masseuse, your hairdresser or your tennis instructor.

If you love to go for a drive—love and go for a drive.
So do you like to go for a drive? Then slide to hell.

It's necessary to pay for songs under playback by money X-copies.

I want a baby very much . . . A girl . . . Eighteen years old!

—I want such a love like in a fairy tale!
—With a prince?
—No, with a happy end.
['end' also means a male intimate organ in Russian slang]

I want to know if love is wild, I want to know if love is real.

I wish for a belt for the world champion of boxing instead of a belt of fidelity.

I wish that we would be equal but not the same.

I wish you health in your personal life!

I would rather sit on a pumpkin and have it all to myself than be crowded on a velvet cushion.

Limit all U.S. politicians to two (2) terms:
One in office and one in prison!
Illinois did that already.

Low-alcohol drinks—for weak alcoholics!

May the sun in his course visit no land more free, more happy, more lovely, than this our own country!

Man is praying:

—My God, what is one million years for you?

—One instant!

—And what is one million dollars for you?

—One penny!

—So give me this penny!

—Well! Wait one moment . . .

My God, if you have already made so that I'm not able to have a sex then make so that I wouldn't want it.

Never say 'NEVER'.

And never say other words too.

And, in general, SHUT UP!

"Sleep on your back is harmful to your lungs, sleep on your stomach is harmful for your intestines, sleep on your left side is harmful for your heart, and sleep on your right side is harmful for your liver."

Magazine 'Health' wishes you pleasant dreams!

My only desire is that everything that I want would be executed.

Today I wish you a day of ordinary miracles,

A fresh pot of coffee you didn't make yourself,

An unexpected phone call from an old friend,

Green lights on your way to work,

The fastest line at the grocery store,

A good sing-along song on the radio,

Your keys found right where you thought you left them.

Vodka? Warm? From a soap tray? Certainly I will!

When will the Lord start to test me for riches?!

Women wish to be virginal, and girls—feminine.

It would be better if mosquitoes sucked fat instead of blood!

WOULDN'T YOU KNOW IT . . .

Crime statistics indicate that Chinese zippers on Turkish jeans save women from being raped!

In the whole world, only Google understands me perfectly.

Money isn't happiness: a man with ten million dollars can be no happier than a person with nine million.

If a crocodile ate your enemy it does not mean that it is your friend.

Even on the highest throne sits an ass.

Civilization led to the fact that it does not matter who is right and who is wrong; what is important is whose lawyer is better.

To become rich, you need three things: intelligence, talent and lots of money.

Time has come when time is already gone . . .

Wife listens to her husband just when he's on the phone with another woman.

Sometimes, someone calls and asks:
—Who is that?
I came up with an ingenious answer which simply confuses a caller:
—Where?

Man never has to complain about two things: his wife and his car.
He chose them himself!

Your whole life is 90% dependent on you, and is only 10% dependent on circumstances that are 99% dependent on you.

Everything that woman does at home is unnoticed.
It becomes visible when she doesn't do that.

Wikipedia: I know everything!
Google: I'll find it!
Facebook: I know everyone!
Internet: Without me you are nothing!
Electricity: Well, well . . .

Pushkin was the first one who had a dream about the Periodic Table but he didn't understand a damn thing . . .

When you need support it turns out that nobody needs you.
But in fact, nobody needs you almost all the time. You just notice it when you need support.

And God said to the people: "Be fruitful and multiply!" And He repeated it three times for the Chinese.

The experience of Ancient Greece and the United States shows that a normal democracy without slaves cannot be created.

A pure conscience is a sign of bad memory.

Census in Russia:
The population in the country is getting smaller, while the population in Moscow is increasing.

We need wine for health, and we need health to drink vodka.

Yesterday Russian astronauts had three spacewalks; twice—because of problems in the bathroom . . .

Nothing is more annoying as the one whom you interrupted continues talking.

Childhood is an age that can be shown on the fingers!

A striptease is a demonstration of eternal values.

Pigeons most honestly express people's attitude to leaders and all of their monuments.

Scientists have found a gene that is responsible for the wish of scientists to find genes.

Business is a game in which the winner is the one who best knows the rules, and the loser is the one who follows them.

A nervous person is not the one who knocks his fingers on the table but the one who is annoyed by it.

No matter how much vodka you drink, your body still consists of 70% of water!

Man spends 30% of his life in sleep. The remaining 70% of his life he dreams of a good sleep.

An intellectual is the one who can find an activity that is more interesting than sex.

A smart woman never yells at man . . . Orders are said calmly, clearly and concisely!

There are no healthy people—there are unexamined people!

Beer comes out of the body faster than coffee or milk because its color change is not necessary. And some sorts of domestic beer are even faster than, say, Czech, Danish, and German beers because their taste change is also not necessary.

If you have a headache that means you have a head.

Those who find an exit are trampled first.

Our athletes are easily recognizable by the yellow singlet and the blue underpants, other skiers dressed a little warmer.

A drop of nicotine kills a horse, and breaks a hamster into pieces!

A head is good . . . but along with a body it's much better.

Unattended small children become young parents very quickly.

Any working day shortens your life by 8 hours.

Russian language without illegal words turns into a report.

It's difficult during treatment but it's much easier to lay in the grave.

The media says that a very large oil reserve has been found in Antarctica. The bloody regime of penguins will soon come to an end.

Usually, girls love dolls and boys—nice cars. But this is the only up to 17 years old. After that age everything is the opposite.

Light travels faster than sound. That's why some people show up before they are heard.

We never really grow up—we only learn how to act in public.

War does not determine who is right—it only determines how many people are left alive.

The evening news begins with 'Good Evening' and then continues by telling you why it isn't.

Stealing ideas from one person is plagiarism.
Stealing ideas from many people is research.

A bus station is where a bus stops.
A train station is where a train stops.
There is a work station on my desk.

You never know what to expect from a woman . . . a boy or a girl.

All that is good in life is illegal, immoral, or leads to obesity.

There are days when you are a pigeon, and there are days when you are a monument.

The probability of a big winning in a lottery is always the same and doesn't depend on whether you bought a lottery ticket or not.

Scientists say that a human body grows only up to 25 years.
But your stomach and butt probably do not know that . . .

Russia is one of the countries where there's the highest number of alcoholics in winter time. Egypt, Turkey, Cyprus and Thailand have the highest number of alcoholics during the time of holiday season!

Everything is said after the fifth glass—'information leakage'.

All traffic inspectors usually ask: "Have you been drinking?"
And no one is interested in: "Did you eat?"

Man is usually much smarter than is necessary for his happiness.

The goal or target determine the caliber.

The first one who greets is the one with weaker nerves.

Fairy tales are the scary stories that carefully prepare children for reading newspapers and watching TV news.

A man who accepts his mistake when he is wrong is a wise man.
A man who accepts his mistake when he is right is the one who is married.

If you help your friend in trouble he always thinks of you when he gets into trouble once again.

The surest way to force your wife listen to you carefully is to talk in sleep.

Experience is a mass of valuable knowledge on how not to behave in situations that would never happen again.

If your relatives or friends don't phone you for a very long time then they are OK.

It's not enough to know how much you cost—you should be in demand.

If a woman says "NO" then she just wants to talk!

—

If you have a wonderful wife, drop dead lover, cool car, no problems with the authorities and tax authorities, and when you go out into the street the sun always shines, and you smile at passers-by—say "NO" to drugs.

Money cannot buy happiness but, somehow, it's more comfortable to cry in a Mercedes-Benz than it is on a bicycle.

Many people are alive only because it's illegal to shoot them.

Childhood is when sleep is not a dream but a duty.

People behave wisely only when they exhausted all other possibilities.

Terrible injustice: nerve cells do not regenerate, and fat cells do not disappear!

The secret of success in life is associated with integrity and honesty:
If you do not have these qualities—your success is guaranteed!

The source of our wisdom is our experience. The source of our experience is our stupidity.

The quieter the pool—the more professional the devils in it!

It turns out that giraffes need a long neck to spy on the squirrels in the hollows.

Pure conscience is a sign of bad memory.

It's better to have a belly from drinking beer than a hump from the job.

A woman's final decision is rarely the last one.

People usually marry his/her hopes and promises.

Practice is when everything works but it's not clear how.
Theory is when everything is clear but nothing works.
Yet, sometimes theory and practice are combined: nothing works and nothing is clear.

Maturity is the age when we are still young, but with much more difficulty.

Just a few men know how to correctly give their hand to a lady who gets out of a cellar with a sack of potatoes!

You cannot be cheerful, sober and intelligent at the same time.

It is found that bachelors bring more money to family than married men.

Every cigarette you've smoked shortens your life by 2 hours,
Each bottle of vodka you've drunk reduces your life by 3 hours,
Every working day shortens your life by 8 hours.

Sometimes a good mood is transmitted only in the sexual way.

A balanced diet is when you are holding in each hand pieces of exactly the same cake.

Even in the worst person can you find something good if he is thoroughly searched.

School is a place where teachers require that students know all subjects while they really know just one.

Objective reality is a delirium caused by lack of alcohol in your blood.

Friends are the people who know you well but still love you.

You should never trust a woman who doesn't conceal her age.
Women who can do this are capable of anything!

A successful marriage is when there is an opportunity to have a mistress, and there is no desire.

Love is when looking bad is not terrible.

Every woman wants a new dress. But more frequently she wants to fit into the old one.

The biggest misconception of women "He will change!"
The biggest mistake men make: "She's not going anywhere!"

In order to kill time, you don't even need to aim.

Leadership of the country should be given to a proctologist. He will also do everything through the asshole but at least professionally.

We become mature not when we no longer listen to mother but when we realize that mom was right!

We live for those who need us, make friends only with those in whom we believe, communicate with those who are pleasant, and are grateful to those who appreciate!

Only money ends faster than the weekend!

A hamster that weighs about 40 pounds belongs to a girl who is the most caring person in the world!

Swiss researchers found that chocolate improves mood—they probably didn't try vodka.

There are two possible scenarios in Russia: WORST and MOST UNLIKELY.

The exodus of Jews out of the country leads to the collapse of the empire (Egyptian folk superstition).

A married woman is the one who has a great future behind her.

The law of life: the strong eat the tasty.

In Russia, if something is done by a key that is less than #24 is considered as nanotechnology.

Alarm clock helps you sometimes to wake up but basically it disturbs your sleep.

Vodka with ice harms the kidneys, rum with ice harms the liver, gin with ice harms the heart, and whiskey with ice harms the brain. Damn, ice is incredibly harmful.

Maturity is an age when a person ceased to grow vertically and began to grow horizontally.

The Russian spy *Petrov*, who fluently speaks five languages, instantly was identified and arrested when someone stepped on his leg in the subway.

If you can laugh at your troubles, you will always have a reason to laugh.

When a person drinks he becomes a different person. But this different person also wants to drink.

The length of a minute depends on which side of the bathroom door you are on.

Happiness is when people talk about you the only good, and you're still alive.

Some people become smarter over the years, while others get older . . .

He was ready to die for love, but she took only cash.

Due to the financial crisis, the light at the end of the tunnel will be turned off to save energy.

Alfred Nobel who invented dynamite is considered to be the first one for the simple reason: the previous inventors had not been identified.

They say that dogs are smarter because they are trainable, but actually cats are smarter because they are not amenable to training.

Due to the cold weather in Russia the number of paved roads has greatly increased.

Vodka is a psychotherapist who is working 24 hours a day and 7 days a week.

They say German quality (made in Germany) does not compare with Chinese quality . . .
Nonsense! The Great Wall of China is standing for two thousand years and will be standing. The Berlin Wall stood for just a half a century.

If mom thinks that you eat a lot and sleep a lot, so it's not your mother—it's your wife's mother.

According to a poll, 38% of Russians believe the country is moving in the wrong direction. The remaining 62% believe that the country is not going anywhere at all.

Only when a liquor bottle drops on asphalt do you realize how little you know about the Russian language.

Swine flu is flu when these pigs do not even phone you to find out if you're still alive.

There is just one measure of health in Russia—you drink or you don't.

Ballroom dancing is the art of moving your feet faster than your partner step on them.

The speed of sound is a very strange physical parameter. Your parents told you something at 20 years, and you begin to understand it only at 40.

All people bring happiness, but some by their presence and others by their absence.

Moldovan scientists have decoded traffic signals.

Once a famous Russian explorer *Przewalski* met a horse . . . A year later she took his name.

It is impossible to forbid living beautifully. But it can be disturbed . . .

Plants are useful: they produce oxygen that is vital for cars.

It is better to sweat seven times than be frozen once!

There are their own charms at every age but at a young age there also are the other charms.

The best alibi is being a victim.

When time is short, there is no place for friendship—only love.

Wisdom does not always come with age. It happens that age comes alone.

It is difficult to fight with excess weight if you are in the same weight class with it.

Solving a crossword is the best way to prove that there is a heap of unnecessary information placed in your head.

All of us will pass through the Last Judgment. Therefore, even in paradise all of us will have at least one previous conviction.

Only a Russian man can bet on a case of vodka that he will stop drinking.

While we complain about life, it passes by . . .

Switzerland could fit seven times in the Tyumen region (Siberia), but it does not want to.

Only in Russia, if you ask a man: "Where are you going?" You get the answer: "I'll be right back."

The most dangerous kind of lie is a not completely said truth.

The economic situation is now so serious that women marry for love.

Most stupid things are done during a day when a person gets up early and goes to bed late.

The meaning of life is necessary in order to have something to think about while sitting on the toilet bowl.

The older an archaeologist's wife, the more he loves her.

Optimists believe in a happy doomsday.

Politicians come and go, but their promises live forever.

Money is not happiness! Happiness is in love! In simple, ordinary, human love of money.

A young queen had a headache all the time because her head grew up, and her crown did not.

Intelligence is a disgusting thing! People without brains are absolutely sure of their high level of intelligence. Clever people are well aware that they are, in essence, morons . . .

You have a successful career if the number of people you can dismiss far exceeds the number of people who can fire you.

An athlete in diving forgot to tighten his swimming trunks—he didn't get the prize but received the Audience Award.

Only a mother can learn to OVERCOME THE IMPOSSIBLE: "Shut your mouth and eat your soup!"
RESPECT WORK OF OTHERS: "If you're going to kill each other, go to the street because I just washed the floor!"

BELIEVE IN GOD: "Pray that this dirty stuff washed off"!"

THINK LOGICALLY: "Because I said so, that's why!"

THINK ABOUT CONSEQUENCES: "If you drop out of the window, I won't take you with me to the store!"

If a dog bites a postman it is not interesting to the media.

If, on the contrary, the postman bites the dog, it's sensational and is interesting to the media.

People are much smarter than they need to be happy.

He who recognizes his mistake when he's wrong is wise.

He who recognizes his mistake when he's right is married.

The only man who could do whatever he wanted with *Natasha Rostova* was the famous Russian writer *Leo Tolstoy*.

He gave a concert for the starving African children.

That's right! Let the children of Africa know that there are things that are more terrible than hunger!

Smart people are those who earn money using their heads, and wise-ones for which these smart people work.

Alcohol kills nerve cells. Only quiet cells remain.

The Bible teaches us how to live, and Criminal Code specifies the details.

Life is beautiful and amazing—you only need to choose the right antidepressant.

—

Lottery—the most accurate way to measure the number of optimists.

The extreme degree of amnesia is when you're standing next to the bathroom door, holding the door handle and thinking if you're going there or leaving from there . . .

People who do morning exercises die a hundred times less than people who don't.
Because the number of people who do morning exercises is a hundred times less than the rest of the people.

When God created man He did not patent his invention. Now any fool can do the same thing.

The first marriage is for love, the second one is based on calculation, and the third is related to habit.

Due to the negligence of Hermitage employees the painting by Kazimir Malevich's "Black Square" was hanging upside down for two months.

Soccer is when everyone is watching 22 millionaires who are playing with a ball.

The best way to create a small business: buy a big business and be patient . . .

Marriage is not a lottery. In a lottery you have a chance.

People are always sincere when they are mistaken and are doing something wrong.

Life as a toilet paper roll: it is lengthy, but sometimes it is spent on shit.

If a person talented, he is talented in almost everything. There is the same situation with idiots.

Yes, time heals. But the outcome is always fatal.

The wedding night is nothing compared to the first extramarital night.

Through the years, the chance of love until death is greatly increased . . .

The mood is always better after sex!
The conclusion is clear: good mood is sexually transmitted!

Each person is endowed with a brain, but not all understand the user' instructions.

—What is discipline?
—It is the art to always be more stupid than your boss.

The facts:
—If a walk is so good for the health, the postman would be immortal!
—A whale swims all day, eats only fish, drinks only water . . . And it is thick!
—A rabbit runs, jumps, and is a vegetarian but it lives only 8 to 10 years!
—A turtle does not run, does not jump, always comes last, and is never in hurry and it lives 250 years.
Conclusion: Forget sport and diet!

Theory teaches us to see far ahead, and practice to watch your step.

Life is always worse than you want it to be, but it's better than it sounds.

'Greenpeace' released a fly swatter "Give a fly a chance" with a hole of 1cm x 1 cm.

Only in Russia you can look at a stripper with pedagogical education.

The computer has a distinct advantage compared to the brain—it is used.

The odds of winning the lottery will increase very slightly if you buy a lottery ticket.

Previously, there was the exploitation of man by man, and now it is the other way around.

Wouldn't you know it . . . ? Brain cells come and brain cells go, but FAT cells live forever.

A gossipmonger is the one who talks to you about others.
A downer is the one who talks to you about himself.
A brilliant conversationalist is the one who speaks to you only about you.

Three basic genetic traits have been transferred from ape to man:
Desire to make jokes.
Desire to climb higher.
Lack of desire to work.

People, who have a lot of money, are either guarded by the police or pursued by the police.

The erudite man is a man who will always find a synonym, if he doesn't know how to spell the word.

Children's wisdom: if Mom laughs at Dad's jokes, there are guests in the house.

A man is closest to perfection in those moments when he fills in the questionnaire when applying for a job.

Force—in beer,
health—in wine,
nobility—in cognac,
germs—in water . . .

Progress of civilization—making more accurate tools more accurate . . .

Striptease is a demonstration of eternal values.

Business is a game in which the winner is the one who best knows the rules, and the loser is the one who performs them.

Parenting is the process of removing your personal flaws from your children.

A smart man always knows what he wants, but a wise man also knows why he needs it.

By finding riches you lose conscience, by finding a woman you are losing your mind, by finding the truth you are losing faith . . . and only after losing everything you find freedom.

It turns out that all dinosaurs were the same; it's just that different archaeologists assembled them in different ways.

Painting is a profession—to sell the paintings is an art.

The word 'NO' is still one of the most effective means of contraception.

Those who have brains and communication skills go into business. Those who have brains, but no communication skills go into science. Those who have communication skills, but no brains go into politics.

A minimum wage guarantees a minimum life expectancy.

Life is divided into three periods:

1. When we believe in Santa Claus.
2. When we do not believe in Santa Claus.
3. When we become Santa Claus.

Time is the best teacher. Unfortunately, it kills all pupils.

When there is no choice, as a rule, the most correct decision is accepted.

Dandruff is sawdust of horns that cut away.

"My grandmother started walking five miles a day when she was sixty. She's ninety-seven now, and we don't know where the heck she is."

In addition to fools and poor roads, Russia has another ailment—fools giving directions at crossroads.

The condom does not guarantee complete security. One of my friends put it on and was still hit by a car.

The horse is the only animal into which you can hammer nails.

A real intellectual is a person who thinks a lot about what does not concern him.

A real music fan hears a woman's voice crooning in the bathroom, bends down to the keyhole and puts his ear to it!

According to statistics a car hits a person every three seconds in New York. Poor guy just cannot get up . . .

Clever and Cute

How does Moses make his tea? Hebrews it.

Venison for dinner again? Oh deer!

A cartoonist was found dead in his home. Details are sketchy.

I used to be a banker, but then I lost interest.

Haunted French pancakes give me the crêpes.

England has no kidney bank, but it does have a Liverpool.

I tried to catch some fog, but I mist.

They told me I had type-A blood, but it was a Type-O.

I changed my iPod's name to Titanic. It's syncing now.

Jokes about German sausage are the wurst.

I know a guy who's addicted to brake fluid, but he says he can stop any time.

I stayed up all night to see where the sun went, and then it dawned on me.

This girl said she recognized me from the vegetarian Club, but I'd never met herbivore.

When chemists die, they barium.

I'm reading a book about anti-gravity. I just can't put it down.

I did a theatrical performance about puns. It was a play on words.

PMS jokes aren't funny; period . . .

Why were the Indians here first? They had reservations.

We're going on a class trip to the Coca-Cola factory. I hope there's no pop quiz.

I didn't like my beard at first. Then it grew on me.

Did you hear about the cross-eyed teacher who lost her job because she couldn't control her pupils?

When you get a bladder infection urine trouble.

Broken pencils are pointless.

What do you call a dinosaur with an extensive vocabulary? A thesaurus.

I dropped out of communism class because of lousy Marx.

All the toilets in New York's police station have been stolen. The police have nothing to go on.

I got a job at a bakery because I kneaded Dough.

Velcro—what a rip off!

Printed in Great Britain
by Amazon.co.uk, Ltd.,
Marston Gate.